Books to Grow By

Bob Keeshan, TV's "Captain Kangaroo"

illustrated by Kyle Corkum

**Fairview
Press**
Minneapolis, Minnesota

BOOKS TO GROW BY ©1996 Robert Keeshan.
All rights reserved. No part of this publication may be used or repro-
duced in any manner whatsoever without written permission, except
in the case of brief quotations embodied in critical articles and
reviews. For further information, please contact the publisher.

Library of Congress Cataloging-in-Publication Data

Keeshan, Robert.
        Books to grow by / Bob Keeshan ; illustrated by Kyle Corkum.
            p.   cm.
        Includes index.
        ISBN 0-925190-83-7 (alk. paper)
        1. Children—Books and reading.   2. Children's literature—
Bibliography. I. Corkum, Kyle, ill. II. Title.
Z1037.K33   1996
[PN1009.A1]
028.1'62—dc20   95-44273
                                                      CIP

Research by Monica Walsh.
Cover art and interior illustrations by Kyle Corkum.
Cover design and page layout and composition by
Circus Design.

First Printing: January 1996
Printed in the United States of America

00 99 98 97 96   7 6 5 4 3 2 1

Published by Fairview Press, 2450 Riverside Avenue South,
Minneapolis, MN 55454.

For a current catalog of Fairview Press titles, please call this
Toll-Free number: 1-800-544-8207

Publisher's Note: Fairview Press publishes books and other materials related to the subjects of
physical health, mental health, chemical dependency, and other family issues. Its publications,
including *Books to Grow By*, do not necessarily reflect the philosophy of Fairview Hospital and
Healthcare Services or their treatment programs.

The paper used in this publication meets the minimum requirements of American National
Standard for Information Sciences—Permanence of Paper for Printed Library Materials, ANSI
Z329.48-1984.

Table of Contents

Books, Stories, Computers, and Reading

H uman beings are marvelous creatures!
Among the many species sharing this earth, human beings have an intelligence that allows for communication on a high plane. Many other species communicate, but few in the intelligent way humans do. An essential element in our ability to express ourselves is the use of language. We enter this world as infants, able to communicate in only limited ways. As we mature, normal development leads to the use of language, to which the skill of reading is basic.

Adults, particularly parents, are key in this process. A parent teaches a child many things in a child's "voyage of discovery," that process by which all children learn the incredible bulk of knowledge necessary to grow and to live in a society. Parents and other adults are a child's guide to life-skills that enable a child—eventually and ironically— to function without assistance from parents.

In reading to a child from infancy, adults do several things. They make books and stories an important part of a child's life. They also spend time with a child. A message of self-worth is sent every time a parent spends time reading to a child. "This most important person in my life is spending time with me, therefore I must be of value." No more important message can be sent.

I often talk about "telling a story," rather than "reading a story." Not all stories are read from books, and storytelling is appropriate at story time. One example is telling "goofy stories," always a fun and empowering experience for a child (see pages 16-19). You'll soon make up your own goofy stories and delight your listeners and yourself!

Conversation is an important aspect of story time. Asking questions and discussing meanings are important intellectual challenges for a child and are intimately associated with reading at all ages.

Books to
Grow By

A powerful form of storytelling is oral history. Children are fascinated by tales from the childhood of a parent or other adult. When I meet parents and children at book signings or other occasions, parents will often say to a child, "I grew up with this man when I was little." Almost always I see a smile, a sparkle in the eyes of the child as she/he looks up to the parent, enchanted by the notion of Mommy or Daddy being little. This is an important link for a child, a confirmation, in a sense, that they, too, will grow and someday be adults. Oral history also serves to "connect" a child to family and its various components, grand-parents, cousins, aunts, uncles.

Please take seriously the value of bringing the child and adult together at story time. I have adults tell me how important my television story times were to them and how they fostered a bond between us. The adult, particularly the parent, enjoys a great opportunity to build a bond with a child and to pass on family values and societal values. Provide a regular time in your busy life for a story time and respect the great importance of that schedule to a child and to you. After all, why are we so busy if not to provide for the healthy development of our families?

Reading is important, but it should also be fun. Don't make reading feel like work, or a task. An objective in reading to a young child is to foster a love of reading that will last a lifetime. Forcing a child to read before that child is ready is counterproductive. When reading-readiness comes to a child, that child will read—if he or she has not been pushed and had reading become onerous. Recent studies indicate that children pushed to read before they are ready are not as accomplished at it as children who have been allowed to read when they choose.

Many fans of new technology believe that computers will make reading books obsolete. They often express this opinion in a book or magazine. The computer and other new technologies are marvelous, but they are tools, after all, just like books. We need reading skills to utilize these tools. I see little difference between searching for information in a printed or a CD-ROM encyclopedia. Technology is marvelous and enables great adventures for everyone. But reading is as basic to the use

of these technologies as it is basic in the use of books.

When driving an auto from New York to San Francisco, a road map is a useful tool. In teaching a child language and reading, this book should prove useful as a "road map," a reference guide for selecting materials for a child at every stage of development.

We are fortunate to have so many fine juvenile books available in the English language. I have reviewed a small number of those, including those I particularly favor or have enjoyed over the years. This guide summarizes those books and classifies them according to age appropriateness and values they teach. There are many other books as well, and this guide will help you choose books with which you and your child can enjoy happy and productive story times.

This volume was written as a reference work for every family library. You may visit a book store and buy the books mentioned herein. Owning books and building a library is important to a child but not critical. The public or school libraries in your community can provide most of these books to read and return for others to enjoy. Building a cherished library for a child has value, but reading the book is most important.

Books are basic to intelligent life. I hope you will find this guide, this road map to parenting, useful in bringing joy and knowledge to your young person. I hope that this volume will be your parent's, grandparent's, adult guide to "books to grow by."

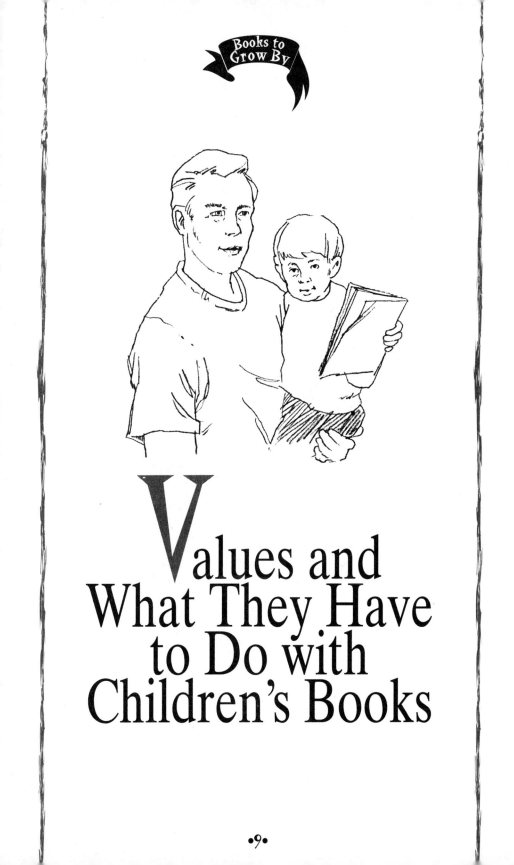

Values and What They Have to Do with Children's Books

No matter what form they take—books, family oral history, or made-up tales—the stories we tell children are a major way of handing down our particular history, our culture, and our values to the next generation.

When we tell family stories, children are linked to other family members, cousins, grandparents, aunts, uncles. As family history connects children to their families, the stories we read to children connect them to the wider human family. We read to our children to set the stage for their reading success, to foster a closeness between parent and child, and to link children to some experience in the larger world. Their "voyage of exploration" enlarges their world beyond the physical contacts they have known.

As parents, one of our principal functions is the giving of values. Just as we place healthy food on the table to foster strong bodies, so we foster strong minds and characters by the menu of values we place before our children. The values we choose to teach our children are lived out in the wider experiences that can be found in the stories we tell and the books we read with our children. I've included values in this guide to assist parents, guardians, grandparents, aunts, uncles, teachers, etc., to choose books not only for the wonderful stories they tell, but also for the values they share.

Many values are found in these books. I have chosen to focus on six of them. You will, no doubt, be able to pick out many more that you feel are important to highlight for your children. Departing from the story for discussion of a value can emphasize its importance. This way you will not only help your child to read and enhance your relationship, but you will also share values you feel are essential. No matter what happens in school, parents are natural teachers, and story time has been, through the ages, a time for that teaching.

IMAGINATION

What would childhood be without imagination? What would our lives as adults be without imagination? Imagination is critical to success in life, regardless of your chosen field. Far too many adults associate imagination with the arts, writing, painting, acting. But imagination is critical in the sciences, in business, in education, in any field. Perhaps the greatest imaginative mind of this century belonged to Albert Einstein, a scientist who imagined what might be with little reference to known knowledge at the time.

Imagination begins in childhood, and it is critical that adults foster imagination in children. Creativity, resourcefulness, thinking with an active mind, creating something never before dreamed of—that's imagination with a capital "I." Some examples:

• Introduce your child to Harold in *Harold and the Purple Crayon.* Notice how Harold can create a whole world with his big purple crayon.

• Another imaginative boy is Max in *Where the Wild Things Are.* Max creates a world of adventure as a way to deal with being sent to his room. As adults, many people use fantasy in a healthy manner to deal with conflict, disappointments, and challenges.

• *What Do You Do with a Kangaroo?* uses imagination to solve many challenges. As adults, we use imagination every day in problem solving.

• The sisters in *Lon Po Po: A Red Riding Hood Story from China* need not only courage to deal with the danger confronting them, but also imagination to come up with a solution that will work the first time.

SELF-DISCIPLINE

Every parent wants to see self-discipline in children as they grow. I see self-discipline as the ability to be in charge of oneself, to make decisions based on values we have internalized from our parents. As parents, we cannot follow children through life. From preschool on,

children are away from their parents more and more. As I tell parents in my seminars, "Successful parenting is teaching children to do without parents." Ironic as it may seem, as parents we work toward that objective, and that objective comes with self-discipline.

Self-discipline plays a big part in reaching goals and in improving skills, whether finishing a homework project or learning a better baseball throw. Self-discipline requires perseverance, controlling impulses, balancing needs, delaying gratification, and being able to cooperate. Because this is often perceived as work by children, they need to see the rewards it can bring.

• Younger children will share the delight of *The Little Engine that Could* when it reaches its goal, because they will be right there pulling the train up the mountain. The little engine achieves its goal through positive thinking and never giving up—a message not lost on children.

• The title character, Grace, in *Amazing Grace* shows everyone that she won't be bound by other people's opinions. Encouraged by her mother and grandmother, Grace concentrates on what she needs to do to realize her goals.

• Even in the classic fairy tale *The Three Little Pigs,* the pig who is safe from the wolf is the one who took the time to build a house strong enough to withstand "the huff and the puff."

TRUSTWORTHINESS

How can you have a relationship without trust? For an infant trust is basic. The question "Can I trust those around me to feed, clothe, and love me?" is of great importance. As the child grows, trust expands from meeting basic needs to questions of honesty, dependability, truthfulness, and respect for self and others. Trust becomes a basic ingredient in family relationships, friendships, school and work relationships.

• Children need to trust those around them and to feel trusted. Stories such as *On Mother's Lap, The Runaway Bunny, On the Day You Were Born,* and *Storm in the Night* highlight the feeling of trust children feel

when those around them respond to and love them.

• Trust is woven into the friendships in *George and Martha, Harriet and Walt, Frog and Toad Are Friends,* and *Rosie and Michael.* Children see how important honesty and dependability are in a friendship and what can happen when they are missing.

• *The Three Bears, Red Riding Hood,* and *The Tale of Peter Rabbit* are three classics where trustworthiness is key to the story.

• In *Mirette on the High Wire,* Mirette re-establishes another person's self-confidence through her own self trust.

• In the story of *Gluskabe and the Four Wishes,* honesty and dependability result in the highest rewards.

FAIRNESS

"But that's not fair!" is a sentence heard often by most parents. Fairness is very important to children; they want things to be fair. Candy will be counted or divided to its most precise degree to make sure everyone gets the same amount. Parents' attention will be watched to make sure that each child gets equal time. For older children, rules in a game are haggled over and hammered out to ensure that they are fair to everyone. What's fair from a child's point of view centers on what he or she is getting or not getting in the situation. But children must know that fairness also includes honesty and compassion, understanding and empathy, and the ability to look at something from the other person's point of view.

• In *Noisy Nora,* Nora has her own view about what is fair in her family.

• The classic tale *The Little Red Hen* shows the little hen dealing with fairness and the meaning of "friends."

• Arthur in *Arthur's Baby* has to deal with his own feelings of what's fair when a new baby comes into the family, a frequent family situation when a new baby intrudes on a previously exclusive relationship.

• In *An Enchanted Hair Tale,* Sudan has to deal with being treated unfairly because of who he is. Children familiar or unfamiliar with this

behavior will find this an important story.
• The old turtle in the book *Old Turtle* has valuable lessons to share on the ideas of fairness, compassion, and understanding.
• In *Old Henry*, a whole neighborhood has to examine its notion of fairness when one of its residents moves away.

COURAGE

Children often think of courage as physical strength and need to learn that it is an internal quality. Courage is the strength to meet danger or hardship, the ability to persevere in difficult situations. Courage means standing up for oneself or someone else, or admitting when you are wrong. Courage is the quality that will enable a child to do what is right.
• In the classics *Katy and the Big Snow*, *Mike Mulligan and His Steam Shovel*, and *The Little Engine that Could*, all the main characters have the courage to persevere when the going gets tough.
• In *Abuela's Weave* and *The Whispering Cloth*, grandmothers and their granddaughters share great lessons of courage.
• Children need courage to face common fears in *What's under My Bed?* and *Harry and the Terrible Whatzit*.
• *The Legend of the Bluebonnet* relates the tale of a young girl's courage and sacrifice for her people.
• Many people follow their dreams with great courage, as in *Follow the Drinking Gourd* and *Wagon Wheels*.

GENEROSITY

Ever met a two-year-old who likes to share toys? Not likely. Learning to share is a difficult and important element in "socializing" a young child. Generosity includes caring for others, kindness, compassion, and, at an older age, civic mindedness. Generosity is highly valued in many cultures. It keeps us from becoming a group of individuals only out for ourselves. It is the important social glue that keeps our families cohesive, our communities caring, and our society connected. Without generosity, we could not have families, communities, a nation. A bleak thought.

• In *Make Way for Ducklings,* traffic comes to a stop and cooperates for the well-being of a family of ducklings.

• A grandmother, mom, and daughter show their love for each other, their caring, their need for family in *A Chair for My Mother.*

• A little boy shows compassion and concern for an animal that should scare him in *The Bear's Toothache.*

• *The Elves and the Shoemaker* is a classic story of generosity.

• In *Miss Rumphius,* children can see the effect that one generous person can have on her community.

• Many lessons of generosity appear in the story of *Chin Yu Min and the Ginger Cat.*

You will find other values in many books and stories. It is important to remember that story time is an excellent time for you to give values to children. Over time, many of your values and the values of our civilization will be understood and adopted by the children to whom you read and tell stories. This passing on of values is a key to successful parenting.

Goofy Storytelling, or Mixing It Up

Adults are often frustrated when children ask for the same story for the umpteenth time. "Surely you must be tired of that story after hearing it so many times." Not so. Children love familiarity; it breeds security. Children are empowered when they know a story so well they can recite it from memory. The frustration this can cause in parents can actually lead to delightful story times. When a child asks for an often-read or often-told story, an adult can play a game with a child. Not all stories come from the written page. Adults often tell "stories" from memory because they are so well known.

A child who knows a story well will find great mastery in correcting a mistake, even the smallest mix-up in the latest telling. An example of this technique is shown in the following story, "Marty MixUp and the Bears." Try being your own Marty MixUp with a story or book familiar to a child. The child will feel wonderful that she or he knows more about the story than you do, and you will feel wonderful about the delight you are giving the child.

Here's to happy mix-ups!

MARTY MIXUP AND THE BEARS

Marty MixUp loved his children, all twenty of them.

Or perhaps there were more.

Or perhaps there were less.

Marty MixUp, or Daddy MixUp as his children called him, loved to tell stories.

But Daddy MixUp was always mixed up in telling stories and in everything else.

So Daddy MixUp asked his children to correct him if he should make a mistake.

The children said, "Okay, Daddy MixUp."

"Thank you," said Daddy MixUp.

"You're welcome, Daddy," said the children.

Everyone was very polite in the MixUp home.

That made it a very nice place to live.

Daddy MixUp started the story of "Goldilocks and the Three Bears."

Everyone knows that story.

Everyone except Daddy MixUp.

"Once upon a time," said Daddy, "there was a little girl who went for a walk, and in the middle of the woods she came upon a small house."

"So far, so good, Daddy," said the children.

"Thank you, children," said Daddy.

"You're welcome, Daddy," said the children.

Such a polite home.

Daddy continued, "The little girl's name was Rumplestiltskin . . ."

"No, Daddy MixUp, no! Her name was Goldilocks."

"Of course, children, Goldilocks. After all, this is the story of Goldilocks and the forty bears . . ."

"No, Daddy. Goldilocks and the . . ."

"I remember, children, I remember. Goldilocks and the thirty bears . . ."

"No, Daddy MixUp, no."

"Goldilocks and the twenty bears?"

"No, Daddy MixUp, no."

"Goldilocks and the ten bears?"

"No, Daddy MixUp, no."

"Goldilocks and the five bears?"

"No!"

"Goldilocks and the Chicago bears?"

"No!"

"How many bears were there, children? Show me with

your fingers."

Each child held up three fingers, and Daddy MixUp counted all the fingers.

"Thank you, children. Goldilocks and the sixty bears."

"No, Daddy, just three, three bears."

"Thank you, children. Goldilocks and the three bears. Goldilocks went into the little house and found it empty. There was a small table and on the table were three peanut butter and jelly sandwiches . . ."

"No, Daddy MixUp. Three bowls of porridge."

"Oh, yes. Goldilocks tried the big bowl of porridge and found it too hot. She tried the middle-sized bowl of porridge and found it too cold. She tried the tiny bowl of porridge and found it full of cream cheese and chives . . ."

"No, Daddy MixUp, she found it just right."

"Of course, children, just right. Then Goldilocks went up the tiny stairs and found ninety-seven thousand million trillion beds . . ."

"No, Daddy, three, three beds."

"Right! Three beds each covered with oysters and chocolate sauce . . ."

"No, Daddy MixUp, blankets and sheets."

Just then Mommy MixUp entered the room and said, "Time, children, time. Time to jump in the soup bowl, wet yourself off, and climb under the oysters and chocolate sauce."

"No, Mommy MixUp. Jump in the tub, dry ourselves off, and climb beneath the blankets and sheets."

"Of course," said Mommy MixUp.

"Of course," said Daddy MixUp.

And so, in the happy and polite MixUp home, all the children are sleeping soundly, dreaming dreams. All twenty of the children.

Or are there twenty-nine?

Or are there ninety-seven thousand million trillion children?

But who's counting?

Snore, snore!

Different
Books for
Different
Folks

Children come in different ages and different stages of development. Even at the same chronological age, children may be quite different. Be aware of this and don't stick too strictly to books for the recommended age level. Your child may want a more advanced book, and that's fine, as long as you don't push a child to a more advanced level in an effort to improve reading skills. We know that a child reads best when allowed to be "reading ready." Allow children to set their own rates of reading progress. Ultimately, this practice means children with positive attitudes regarding books and a life-long love of reading.

BIRTH TO TWO YEARS OLD

Some parental comments:

"You're kidding. Read to an infant?"

"Hey, my baby wants to eat books, not read them."

"She's always moving. I can't get her to sit still!"

Baby is settled at home. Now is the time to start reading. Does Baby understand all those words and the story? Of course not. What you read is not as important as the fact that you are reading. Children at any age, even the youngest, grow when they have time with a parent. It is your voice, mother, father, and the sight of your face that Baby enjoys.

These early months are also a good time for songs and nursery rhymes. (They aren't called "nursery rhymes" by accident). All this cre-

ates a bond, a relationship that will enable Baby to develop, emotionally and intellectually. The baby is exploring the use of senses, hearing, sight, speech, touch, taste.

What do touch and taste have to do with books? Baby will want to touch and hold books, and therefore sturdy books are a good idea. In the summaries that follow, I often mention "board books," books with thick, laminated pages made to withstand rough treatment in small hands and even survive some peanut butter and jelly smeared on a page. Handling books is important to a young child. It enhances the familiarity and friendliness of books. They are also good for teething. Oh, what would Johannes Gutenberg have to say about that?

Color and simplicity of pictures are important at this age. Familiar objects like animals are always engaging. Try supplying sounds to go with the pictures—quack quack, woof woof, meow meow, etc. Reach beyond your tonsils for the siren on a fire engine, the rrroar of a truck engine, the whistle of a jet plane. Young children delight in such vocal additions. Loosen up and be "with it" when reading to a child. No need to be embarrassed—your boss isn't listening over your shoulder!

Remember, the relationship between reader and child is very important, so depart from the book for a moment of conversation about the story. Elicit opinions from the child if they have learned to talk. Elicit opinions even if they have not. They will respond with a look or a giggle. Acquiring speech is enhanced when stories and books are introduced at the earliest stage.

Don't be disappointed if Baby leaves your story after a minute or two to explore something else. Attention spans are typically short at a young age, and there's always curiosity about something else. You are establishing stories and books as a fun activity. Never make story time a chore.

Be careful when the child wants to take over and turn pages, often two or three pages at a time. Your creativity in "bridging" the story will make up for multiple turned pages.

Because you have engaged in a story time from the time Baby came home, the day will come when a child will pick up a book and bring it to you for reading. You will probably notice that children often

select books that you have read many times, books that have become their favorites. If you just can't bear to read a story once again, try the goofy storytelling notion (see pages 16-19). It's great fun for all.

A child needs to learn much in these early years. Books and stories are an important part of their development. Make books a part of this process from day one.

TWO TO FOUR YEARS OLD
TWO TO SIX YEARS OLD

Some parental comments:

"My daughter really likes turning pages."

"I'm worried about pages getting torn."

"Can I read the same book to my two-year-old and my four-year-old?"

Once a child has reached the stage where he or she sits with you for a story and brings you books to read, what you read depends on the individual child's interests and activity level. Your child may be interested in something for older children or may want to read something for younger ones. This has nothing to do with the child's intellect; do not draw inferences. Sometimes a child enjoys a book read many times before because it is familiar. Children are creatures of familiarity and find security in knowing what is going to happen on the next page.

Many younger children are fascinated by the pictures in a book for older children and will happily listen as you read to an older child, who enjoys the book on a different level. Some two-year-olds are ready for a picture book with a story, but do remember, attention spans are short at this age and get shorter as the stories get longer. If a child loses interest before a book is finished, that's okay. Every book will be finished eventually, and finishing a book should not, at this age, become a chore. Insisting on such rules at an early age dims the light of reading enjoyment. Keep it fun.

Two- and three-year-olds like simple, repetitive story lines and nice pictures. Read the story to yourself. If you find it dull, chances are the child will also. A story with an often-repeated line such as, "I'll huff and I'll puff," from *The Three Little Pigs,* delights children, and they will want to chime in and become involved. Allow a child to ask questions. Pose questions yourself and keep up the interest of the child. As with an adult reader, reading is an intellectual exercise. Involving a child in the book enhances the intellectual experience.

A child should be taught a respect for books. I can still remember the way my mother handled books with reverence. That feeling for books was transferred to me. A young child will be rough on books—there is simply no way to teach respect at a very early age. That's why we have the "board books" meant to stand up to an infant's rough handling. Nonetheless, respect for books can be shown at the earliest age. With books, as with everything else in the child's life, you are the model. The book handling that you model will not be lost on a child. At this age you may want to keep the "treasured" books on a high shelf, just as you keep the solvents high up and the electric outlets covered, until a child can learn appropriate behaviors.

Many families like to promote activities in which the whole family can join. This is okay for reading time, but be aware that interest levels and attention spans differ greatly in younger and older children. A book with a complicated story line will be lost on a younger child, and one that is too simple will bore an older child. School rooms are separated by grade level for good reason. The same rules apply to reading.

This is a very individualistic activity, and the needs of a particular child must be met at reading time. This does not mean that reading can never be a family activity. There will come times when older children read to younger siblings and when a book is enjoyed by every family member.

THREE TO SIX YEARS OLD
THREE TO EIGHT YEARS OLD

Some parental comments:

"My son wants the same book over and over."

"My child always chooses books at the library that are too difficult."

"Half our books are drawn and scribbled in."

Children are creatures of familiarity. Knowing what is going to happen in a story, as in *Little Red Riding Hood* for instance, gives a child a feeling of power. Keep reading a cherished book, or ask your children to read it to you. They surely know it by heart. Or try the goofy story approach talked about on pages 16-19. A child's feeling of power when you need to be corrected is very healthy.

At this age, books should be everywhere—in the child's bedroom, in your bedroom, in the kitchen, in the car, in the travel bag ready to be pulled out when waiting at the doctor's office.

Establishing a regular reading time gives a child something to look forward to each day, not only for the joy of reading, but just as important, the special time with a parent. If your schedule sometimes gets in the way, a child will understand—children are resilient. But don't make a habit of it. Children grow and develop in every way when they have access to a parent. When you spend time with a child, as when you spend time with a spouse, you send a message. You respect the child, you love the child, you have time for the child. That's how children develop in healthy ways, and that's why special reading times are critical in their lives.

A young child likes to express himself/herself by scribbling. Have some drawing paper handy to satisfy this urge at reading time. Crayons are for drawing paper, not books. After all, a book would look pretty silly hanging on the refrigerator door!

Three-year-olds like stories about situations they face, such as siblings, independence and authority issues, a new baby, moving to a new home. Some fine children's books feature animal characters who face "people" problems.

Books contribute greatly to language development in children. It's okay to question a child during a story. Language is usually pretty sophisticated at this age, and challenging questions make children search

for language to answer. You may improvise or edit the story line to keep a child's interest, but if you find yourself doing this often, you may be a notch above the child's reading level and may wish to try a simpler book. Frustrating reading experiences are counterproductive—reading a book should be enjoyable.

Acquaint a child with one of the greatest joys in any community, the library. Many libraries are wise enough to have a designated children's area, toys for toddlers, story hours. The children's librarian can give you advice on choosing a book appropriate for a child. You can also rely on your own knowledge of the child to select appropriate books. If a child shows interest in a book, accept it. You may know that book is not right for the child, but he or she does have a reason for choosing it. Maybe it's just the way the book feels. That's okay—a child will learn from the experience.

FOUR TO EIGHT YEARS OLD

Some parental comments:
"My daughter knows if I change a word of the story."
"My son is hung up on dinosaurs—we can't get enough books about them."
"These books are so beautifully illustrated."
Children at this age engage you in wonderful conversations and ask questions to which they want satisfying answers. Their world is

changing. Their "voyage of discovery" has become broader, beyond the crib, beyond the playpen, beyond the house itself. They are soaking up experiences in child care, preschool, in neighborhood play. Their imagination blossoms and often seems like reality. They are hungry for knowledge about the whole world. Books written for children of this age reflect this growth. Often they are beautifully illustrated, lush and detailed. Don't allow your eye to miss these treasures.

Four-year-olds still enjoy the pictures in books, but they also want to hear about issues that are increasingly important in their young lives: family, siblings, solving problems, meeting challenges, using imagination, overcoming fears, feeling power, facing power. They like positive resolutions and satisfying endings.

The attention span may have increased at this age, but the story still needs to "move along." Get children involved in the story by asking questions—what's happening? how does this character feel? Unbend and tell them how you feel—they really are interested in hearing your thoughts. Asking questions and involving them will contribute to their self-confidence and positive sense of themselves.

You should have a sense of what interests your child. Find books that support those interests—clouds, plants, dinosaurs, machines, planes, doctors, nurses, lawyers. This is the time to let the child know that books are great places to find out about things. Teach children the rudiments of using research books such as the encyclopedia and the dictionary.

This is a great age to organize a home library. Find a special place or places in the bedroom, living room, or family room for books. Visit the library and find the research books as well as other books.

Parents often ask me, "How do I get my child interested in books? He doesn't seem to want to read. He just watches television." I usually answer with a question, "What was the last book you read?" The response is often, "Oh, well, I'm tired when I get home from work, so I often just sit by the television with dinner." A parent is the most important person in any child's life, and the child watches everything a parent does, listens to everything being said. If books are not important to you,

how are they going to be important to a child who idolizes you? (That's true, though it may not always seem that way). If you spend your time in front of television, don't wonder why your child does the same. Read. Your child will follow your example, as the night follows the day!

Giving books as a gift is a good idea at this age. It demonstrates your respect for the child and your respect for books. Two respects in one!

FIVE TO EIGHT YEARS OLD

Some parental comments:

"Kindergarten!"

"It's hard to find time."

"We like books about other countries, other cultures."

At this age, children really cut loose from the home on their "voyage of discovery." School means many new friends and many adventures. Books will surround them at school as they have at home. They are familiar sights, thanks to you, the parent.

Children this age will enjoy books that are challenging, books that are rich to look at, and books that are simpler, for relaxation. Curiosity will draw them to turning pages in the encyclopedia. Reading with someone is still the way they enjoy books most. Don't let up; continue the reading hour. As always, it is not only the book, but time with the parent that's important.

Reading time becomes especially important as a calm time of

relaxation after a busy day at school or, in your case, at work. It is a time for closeness and love.

Reading fifteen minutes a day, or more, is especially important for children who are learning to read in school. If they have not been pushed or pressured to read before reading-readiness, they will have warm feelings and positive attitudes about books and will be anxious to acquire reading skills.

If at this time you feel that your child may have a problem with reading, now is the time for consultation. Speak to your child's teacher, or the physician if that seems appropriate. Don't guess about things. Seek professional assistance if you feel it's needed.

A wide range of themes is appreciated at this time. Good illustrations are still important, but stories can be more complex, and fairly sophisticated themes are enjoyed. Don't forget humor—at this age, humor is a really big hit. Stories with real children as characters are popular. Problem solving is important.

Folk tales and fairy tales are fun, and those from another culture can be enriching. Many of these tales deal with difficult themes, such as abandonment, jealousy, anger, love, courage. Intrude with conversation in these stories to soften them. Don't overload your child with scary tales. Even I look under the bed before turning out the light!

Your library may give your child his/her very own library card at this age. How better to show that books are important? It might even call for a celebration.

SIX TO EIGHT YEARS OLD

Some parental comments:

"Should I still read to them when they are reading on their own?"

"Should I choose a book on my child's reading level?"

"What about chapter books?"

Don't give up reading to your child because they can read themselves. Read to them now, tomorrow, and into their teens.

Six- to eight-year-olds (and older) will understand a more complex book being read together than they could read on their own. They will benefit from the conversation and questions that arise from the reading. You can try a book that is something of a stretch, but don't be disappointed if interest wanes.

This is a time for a wide range of themes: adventures, fairy tales, stories with fully developed characters, tales from other lands, books with information to be logged away. Don't forget humor.

Illustrations on every page are no longer necessary, but worthwhile art is always enjoyable. The plot lines must be more complex; simpler plots aren't enjoyed as much.

Chapters begin to appear in books for this age group, and beginning with short chapters is a good idea. As the child learns the format of a book with chapters, the organization becomes appreciated.

Learning to read is not easy for many children, and the process requires that they do a lot of school work. You have an important task at this stage. Keep the fun and joy of books in their lives. Read just for fun. Children will occasionally wish to read a paragraph or perhaps a page. Reading together should continue to be enjoyable. Soon children will have met the challenge and accomplished the goal of acquiring those reading skills.

You established the joy of reading in infancy. You continued it through toddler and preschool years. The light ought to be burning brightly by now, and you will have accomplished a great parenting goal. Keep up your reading, modeling that behavior, and continue your reading time. A parent and child never outgrow their need to read together. Only three things need to be done from now on:

1. READ
2. READ
3. READ

Books
for Birth
to 2
Years
Old

All Fall Down

Very young children delight in the game of "all fall down." This is a sturdy book meant to be carried on the "playing field" by the young participants in the game. I have seen toddlers in preschool develop motor skills along with giggles playing the game so well orchestrated in this book. This will be a favorite of young children because the ending, reached so quickly in eight thick pages, is about one of the favorite games of childhood.

Author and Illustrator: Helen Oxenbury
Macmillan, 1987. Boardbook: $6.95

Other books in this series:
Clap Hands; Tickle, Tickle

Other books by this author:
Dressing; Playing; Working; Say Goodnight

Animal Sounds for Baby

Toddlers love baby animals, and they enjoy hearing the sounds, the distinct sounds, of each animal. Once you feel the child has learned the appropriate sound for each animal, pretend to be confused and make wrong sounds for the animals. "The ducks say meow meow." The child will laugh at your confusion and correct you. What a feeling of power you are building in that child! This is a sturdy board book whose rounded corners and thick pages will stand up to the not-so-gentle handling of wee ones.

Author: Cheryl Willis Hudson, Illustrator: George Ford
Scholastic, 1995. Boardbook: $5.95

Other books by this author:
Bright Eyes, Brown Skin; Afro-bets 123 Book; Afro-bets ABC Book

Birth to 2 Years

Big Friend, Little Friend

As adults, we rarely think of physical size as being important, but children are always aware of big and little. This sturdy board book meant for young hands treats the concept of big and little friends in a most delightful way.

Author: Eloise Greenfield
Illustrator: Jan Spivey Gilchrist
Black Butterfly Children's Books, 1991.
Boardbook: $5.95

Other books by this author:
Daddy and I; I Make Music; My Doll, Keshia; Aaron and Gayla's Alphabet Book; Aaron and Gayla's Counting Book; Sweet Baby Coming

Clap Hands

A very young child works hard to develop motor skills, and *Clap Hands* will advance that effort. Children have so much to learn in the first years of life, the very things we adults take for granted. Waving to dad and mom can be a great accomplishment for a child. Notice the smile of joy accompanying this simple gesture. This book encourages a young child learning much about life.

Author and Illustrator: Helen Oxenbury
Macmillan, 1987. Boardbook: $6.95

Other books by this author:
Helen Oxenbury's ABC of Things; Helen Oxenbury's Nursery Story Book; All Fall Down; Tickle, Tickle; I Can; I Hear; I See; I Touch

Good Morning Sun

Those early years are so full of wonder and surprises for a child. Here a young child, or I should say young bunny, views familiar surroundings with "good morning" greetings. It makes for a nice early morning routine any child will enjoy. The pages are sturdy, so allow a young child to finger them, even goo them up with cereal, if they wish. Wipe the pages clean and start a new day.

Author: Harriet Ziefert
Illustrator: Lisa Campbell Ernst
Penguin, 1988. Boardbook: $10.95

Other books by this author:
Bear's Colors; Bear's Numbers; Bear's Shapes; Bear's Weather; All Clean!; All Gone!

Goodnight Moon

This simple work has been enjoyed by millions of children for a half-century. The great green room is filled with reassuring objects for a child ready to drift off to sleep. It is a comfort for children, as any bedtime story should be.

Author: Margaret Wise Brown
Illustrator: Clement Hurd
HarperCollins, 1947. Boardbook: $3.95

Other books by this author:
Big Red Barn; Little Chicken; The Noisy Book; The Quiet Noisy Book; Red Light, Green Light

Happy Babies

Here is a collection of happy babies, toddlers really, and the many activities that give children such joy. Try playing peek-a-boo and clap hands and other games as you read to your toddler. It will bring some giggles and many smiles.

Author: Wendy Lewison
Illustrator: Jan Palmer
Golden Book, 1994. Boardbook: $4.50

Other books by this author:
Baby's First Mother Goose;
Baby Has a Boo-Boo;
Nighty-Night; Boo! Peekaboo;
Happy Thanksgiving

Other early Golden Books include:
What Does Baby Hear?; Nursery Rhymes;
Good Night, Baby

hey, diddle, diddle

Oh, we all know this one by heart—but where did we first hear it? At the side of an adult, perhaps a parent, who delighted us with the simple rhyme. A small child will want to hold this small book and point to the cat, the cow, the dog, the plate, and the spoon. Go ahead, enjoy it for the umpteenth time!

Author and Illustrator: Dianne O'Quinn Burke
RGA Publishing Group, 1994. Boardbook: $3.95

Other books in this series:
wee willie winkie; there was an old woman; itsy-bitsy spider; hush-a-bye, baby

I Love You, Sun
I Love You,
Moon

This is a book of love for the youngest child. Its pages are sturdy for easy handling by young hands and coated for easy cleaning of jam and other stains. So many of our earth's elements are here, as are some fine animals, the sun in the sky, the moon above. Karen Pandell has given us a lovely text, and the masterful Tomie dePaola, who has gifted us with such fine art for children, has done the illustrations. This, as I have said, is a book of love, the love that surrounds us all. Allow your young child to discover this love.

Author: Karen Pandell, Illustrator: Tomie dePaola
Putnam, 1994. Boardbook: $5.95

i See

This is a toddler book for young children exploring many new things about their world each day. From belly buttons to meowing cats, it is a voyage of discovery. The book is sturdy enough for young hands and might be left in the crib after reading at bedtime.

Author and Illustrator: Rachel Isadora
William Morrow, 1985. Boardbook: $6.95

Other books by the same author:
Babies; Bird

Other books in this series:
I Touch; I Hear

Birth to 2 Years

Max's Ride

A sturdy book for the hands of toddlers, this story in the Max series is filled with humor. Read it again and again, and you'll still hear giggles.

Author and Illustrator: Rosemary Wells
Dial Books for Young Readers, 1979.
Boardbook: $4.50

Other books in this series:
Max's New Suit; Max's First Word; Max's Toys; Max's Breakfast; Max's Bath; Max's Bedtime

Moonbear

Moonbear loves the varied phases of the moon, and you will, too. This simple and sturdy book is just right for young minds and young hands.

Author and Illustrator: Frank Asch
Simon & Schuster, 1993.
Boardbook: $3.95

Other books in this series:
Moonbear's Friend; Moonbear's Books; Moonbear's Canoe

Pat the bunny

A very young child is not only maturing intellectually but is also developing the senses, touch, smell, hearing, seeing, taste. This book will delight a youngster because it caters to these senses, especially the sense of touch. Just wait till you see the expressions on children's faces when they pet the bunny!

Author and Illustrator: Dorothy Kunhardt
Golden, 1940. Sturdy book: $7.75

Also see:
pat the cat; pat the puppy

The Pudgy Book of Mother Goose

Introduce your young person to Mother Goose with eight of everyone's favorite rhymes. This book is sturdy enough for toddler hands.

Illustrator: Richard Walz
Putnam, 1984. Boardbook: $2.95

Other Pudgy books include:
Wheels on the Bus; Hippity-Hop;
Guess Who I Love

The Pudgy Where Is Your Nose? Book

In my parenting seminars, I talk about the child on a "journey of discovery." As adults, we know so very much, most of it learned in those first few years of life, on that journey of discovery. The senses, the parts of our bodies, all are being explored by the young child. This little book, designed for tiny hands, helps a toddler with the process of discovery.

Illustrator: Laura Rader
Putnam, 1989. Boardbook: $2.95

Other Pudgy books include:
Pudgy Book of Farm Animals; Pudgy Bunny Book; Mother Hubbard's Cupboard; A Mother Goose Surprise Book

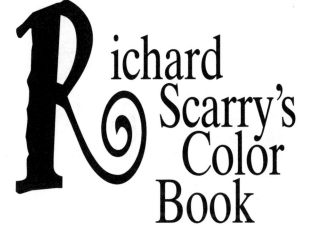

Richard Scarry's Color Book

This is a sturdy board book meant to be placed in very small hands after the reading. It can be studied by a child as he or she is quizzed about the various colors of Mr. Paint Pig. It will not be too long before small ones can name almost a dozen fine colors. This book is just the right level of challenge for a toddler.

Author and Illustrator: Richard Scarry
Random House, 1976. Boardbook: $3.95

Other books by this author:
Richard Scarry's Best Counting Book Ever;
Richard Scarry's Best Word Book Ever;
Richard Scarry's Lowly Worm Word Book;
All About Cars; Early Words; The Three Bears

When It's Time for Bed

This is a sturdy book for young hands and a good checklist on what must be done when it's time for bed. Sleep tight!

Author and Illustrator: Nick Butterworth
HarperCollins, 1994. Boardbook: $4.95

Other books by this author:
Nick Butterworth's Book of Nursery Rhymes; Nice or Nasty: Book of Opposites; Busy People; Making Faces; My Dad Is Awesome; My Mom Is Excellent; My Grandma Is Wonderful; My Grandpa Is Amazing

Birth to 2 Years

Where's Spot?

Young children will delight in looking for Spot. Thanks to the unusual format of this book, a child can join in the search and help to find Spot. They will want the search to begin again. And why not? Find Spot again. And again!

Author and Illustrator: Eric Hill
Putnam, 1980. Boardbook: $4.95

Other books by this author:
Spot Looks at Opposites; Spot Looks at Colors; Spot Looks at Shapes; Spot in the Garden; Spot on the Farm; Spot at Play

Books to
Grow By

Books for 2~4 Years Old

Animal Babies

On "Captain Kangaroo," baby animals were an important part of the program, and the response from parents indicated that children found such juveniles fascinating. Children are growing to maturity just like the baby animals in this book, and the bond between children and baby animals will make this book popular with all youngsters. The illustrations are warm and picture animal families showing great affection, always reassuring to a child. You'll lose your heart to the baby orangutan staring at the butterfly, as well as to the baby ducks and hippos and elephants.

Author and Illustrator: Harry McNaught
Random House, 1977. Paperback: $2.50

Another book by this author:
The Truck Book

Other books in the "Please Read to Me" series:
The Little Puppy; The Little Rabbit;
Kittens Are Like That; Puppies Are Like That

Ask Mr. Bear

Value: Generosity

Danny wants to give his mother something special for her birthday, something she does not already have. The great search begins with the advice of a hen, a goose, a goat, a sheep, and other animals from the farm. Finally, Danny travels over the hill to ask Mr. Bear, who advises him on the very best gift of all for his mother. Guess, if you can, what kind of hug Danny gives his mother.

Author and Illustrator: Margorie Flack
Macmillan, 1932. Paperback: $4.95

Other books by this author:
The Story about Ping; The New Pet; The Restless Robin; Wait for William; Rosie's Walk; The Boats on the River

Bear Shadow

Every young child spends some time fascinated by his/her shadow. This delightful book will help explain a shadow to a child. "Where does my shadow go at high noon?" We learn all about shadows along with Bear.

Author and Illustrator: Frank Asch
Simon & Schuster, 1985. Paperback: $4.95

Other books by this author:
Bear's Bargain; Baby in the Box; Good-bye House; Skyfire; Milk and Cookies; Bread and Honey: A Frank Asch Bear Story; Goodnight Horsey; Just Like Daddy; The Last Puppy

The Big Fat Worm

"The early bird gets the worm." Not in this story about the relationship between different creatures, the worm, the bird, the cat, the dog. The redundancy of language will help a child who is ready to read. The story will delight any young child and should afford a parent a giggle or two.

Author: Nancy Van Laan
Illustrator: Marisabina Russo
Alfred A. Knopf, 1987. Paperback: $4.99

Other books by this author:
Mama Rocks, Papa Sings; Mouse in My House; People, People Everywhere; Tiny Tiny Boy and the Big Big Cow; Round and Round Again; This Is the Hat

2 to 4 Years

The Blanket

Value: Generosity

One of my children, as a toddler, called it a "banky." Different names are assigned to their blanket by different children, but to each the blanket represents security. Many adults find this attachment to a scruffy blanket a mystery. Too bad—they have forgotten their childhood. This lovely story, with a happy ending, relates experiences virtually every parent has faced when the blanket cannot be found. The happy ending? Read the book and you, too, will find the blanket!

Author and Illustrator: John Burningham
Candlewick Press, 1975. Hardcover: $6.95

Other books by this author:
The Baby; The Dog; The Friend; First Steps

2 to 4 Years

Gone Fishing

This is a simple story, but one filled with the warmth of a father-son relationship. It is fun to go fishing with these two, and don't be surprised if your son or daughter wants to go fishing with you, Dad—or with you, Mom! Enjoy the fishing. Bring along a good book in case they're not biting.

Author: Earlene Long
Illustrator: Richard Brown
Houghton Mifflin, 1984. Paperback: $4.95

Another book by this author:
Johnny's Egg

Growing Vegetable Soup

Roll up your sleeves, get ready for fun. Plant the seeds and tend your garden. Children will gain an understanding of what is needed to make things grow. Patience, it takes time—but enjoy the colorful illustrations while waiting. They are as colorful as . . . well, as colorful as vegetables. Into the pot and cook the soup. Mmm, best soup I ever tasted!

Author and Illustrator: Lois Ehlert
Harcourt Brace, 1987. Paperback: $4.95

Other books by this author:
*Planting a Rainbow; Eating the Alphabet:
Fruits and Vegetables from A to Z;
Fish Eyes: A Book You Can Count On*

I Am a Little Bear

Children are intrigued with the similarities between baby animals and themselves. Here a little bear learns about his new world, different than a child's, but familiar in some ways. Except for that long winter's nap!

Author and Illustrator: Francois Crozat
Barron's, 1989. Boardbook: $8.95

Other books in this series:
*I Am a Big Dinosaur; I Am a Little Cat; I Am a Little Dog;
I Am a Little Duck; I Am a Little Monkey; I Am a Little Pig;
I Am a Little Rabbit; I Am a Little Tiger*

2 to 4 Years

Mary Had a Little Lamb

Value: Generosity

This childhood rhyme by Sarah Josepha Hale first appeared in New England early in the nineteenth century. The poem's appearance in McGuffey's Reader helped many American children learn to read. Whatever would Thomas Edison have said on the first phonograph record had this poem not been on his lips?

Author: Sarah Josepha Hale
Photo Illustrator: Bruce McMillan
Scholastic, 1990. Paperback: $4.95

Another book by this author:
Poems for Our Children

Moondance

Value: Imagination

Bear loves to dance, and he would like to dance with the moon. Before you arrive at the last page, Bear will have done quite a bit of dancing.

Author and Illustrator: Frank Asch
Scholastic, 1993. Paperback: $3.95

Other books by this author:
Happy Birthday, Moon; Mooncake; Moongame

On Mother's Lap

Value: Generosity

It seems larger than a great hall, mother's lap. Every young child feels great comfort there and wonders, when a younger baby comes along, whether there will still be room. The book shows a slight touch of sibling rivalry, but soon all is well on mother's lap.

Author: Ann H. Scott
Illustrator: Glo Coalson
Houghton Mifflin, 1992.
Paperback: $5.95

Other books by this author:
Grandmother's Chair; One Good Horse; Someday Rider; Cowboy Country; Hi!; Sam

Peek-A-Boo

Whaat parent hasn't shared the joy of peek-a-boo with a child? Well, here it is between the covers of a book. Children rarely tire of peek-a-boo. Try to see what you will see. Peek-a-boo!

Authors and Illustrators: Janet and Allan Ahlberg
Penguin, 1981. Paperback: $4.50

Other books by these authors:
Bye, Bye Baby; Each Peach Pear Plum; Funny Bones; Jeremiah in the Dark Woods

Pumpkin, Pumpkin

Values: Generosity / Self-discipline

This story shows us the magic of growing things as Jamie plants a pumkin seed and watches the miracle of growth. He enjoys the fruits of his adventure but also plans ahead.

Author and Illustrator: Jeanne Titherington
Morrow, 1986. Paperback: $3.95

Other books by this author:
Baby's Boat; Big World, Small World; Child's Prayer; Sophie and Auntie Pearl; Where Are You Going, Emma?

The Runaway Bunny

Values: Trustworthiness / Generosity

This is the classic tale by Margaret Wise Brown. If you have a child who absolutely needs to "run away," read this one. It may end up with hugs.

Author: Margaret Wise Brown
Illustrator: Clement Hurd
Harper, 1942. Paperback: $3.95

Other books by this author:
*Baby Animals; The Sleepy Little Lion;
Little Chicken; Big Red Barn; Wheel on the Chimney*

Trains

Many children are fascinated by trains. Anne Rockwell's story for the young reader provides not only information, but fun and colorful pictures as well. Toot, toot!

Author and Illustrator: Anne Rockwell
Penguin, 1988. Paperback: $4.50

Other books in this series:
*Big Wheels; Bikes; Boats;
Cars; Fire Engines; Planes;
Trucks*

Books to Grow By

Books for 2~6 Years Old

All about You

Values: Generosity / Imagination

A child will delight in answering the many questions posed in this book. It is well named because it is, indeed, all about you, no matter who you are. There are so many questions and, therefore, so many opportunities for a reader to quiz a child about what they like to do, with whom they enjoy playing, favorite foods, favorite animals, and so much more. The book covers the life and life-styles of every child, and getting the child to make decisions and to express opinions about each choice can lead to giggles and delight. This is a good book for participation and active imagination.

Authors and Illustrators: Catherine and Laurence Anholt
Penguin, 1991. Paperback: $4.99

Other books by these authors:
The Twins, Two by Two; What I Like; One, Two, Three, Count with Me; Bear and Baby

Are You My Mother?

From the Beginner Book series we are presented with this gem. The vocabulary and its redundancy are a splendid introduction for children prepared to read by themselves. This is a cute and often funny book. Children will think much of it is preposterous and that is mighty pleasant reading. Don't push this book on a child who has not yet arrived at "reading readiness," but when a child is ready, this is a good beginning. Besides, it's a great salute to motherhood.

Author and Illustrator: P. D. Eastman
Random House, 1960. Hardcover: $6.95.

Other books by this author:
Best Nest; Big Dog, Little Dog; Flap Your Wings; Go, Dog, Go!; Sam and the Firefly

Clifford the Big Red Dog

This is a dangerous story to read to a child because any child who meets Clifford the Big Red Dog will want a dog like him around the house. That is, if he will fit in the house. Wow, is Clifford big! But he has such a kind heart, and though he sometimes makes mistakes (like the time he fetched a stick that turned out to be the night stick of a policeman with the policeman still attached), he is a nifty companion. The story is a nifty companion, also. You'll want to keep Clifford handy. This BIG dog is good for many BIG smiles!

Author and Illustrator: Norman Bridwell
Scholastic, 1963. Paperback: $2.50

Other books in this series:
Clifford's Good Deeds; Clifford's Tricks; Clifford the Small Red Puppy; Clifford Takes a Trip

The Dinosaur Who Lived in My Backyard

Value: Imagination

Most children pass through a phase when dinosaurs hold great fascination. This child also has a sense of history and the imagination to harness it. At one time, we all had dinosaurs in our backyards who ate lots of vegetables. It was a long time ago, but perhaps they will return. As the story says, save your lima beans!

Author: B. G. Hennessy, Illustrator: Susan Davis
Penguin, 1988. Paperback: $4.99

Other books by this author:
Eeney, Meeney, Miney, Mo; Sleep Tight; Jake Baked the Cake

The Gingerbread Man

Value: Trustworthiness

Another telling of this favorite and, you guessed it, the crafty fox has his way with the Gingerbread Man, right down to the last yummy bite!

Retold and illustrated by: Karen Schmidt
Scholastic, 1967. Paperback: $2.50

Other books by this author:
Chicken Little; The Little Red Hen

Katy and the Big Snow

Value: Self-discipline

Virginia Lee Burton wrote one of my favorites, *Mike Mulligan and His Steam Shovel.* Here she graces us with the adventures of Katy, a beautiful red tractor, who in wintertime sports a snow plow. When the big snow comes, the city is paralyzed, and if it wasn't for Katy, who knows what would happen. It is a difficult job, but Katy perseveres, never giving up—a lesson not lost on young readers.

Author and Illustrator: Virginia Lee Burton
Houghton, 1943. Paperback: $4.95

Other books by this author:
Mike Mulligan and His Steam Shovel; The Little House

Katy No-Pocket

Value: Generosity

How embarrassing, to be a mother kangaroo without a pocket in which to carry your baby. We learn about how many animals carry their babies, and finally Katy solves her no-pocket problem. Such fun.

Author: Emmy Payne
Illustrator: H. A. Rey
Houghton Mifflin, 1944. Paperback: $5.95

2 to 6 Years

Life in the Air

Humans are earth-bound creatures, but throughout our history we have looked to the sky in wonder— wonder about what and who are there and what it would be like to live a life in the air. This work gives us a bird's-eye view of that life from the perspective of a fledgling bird discovering a new life in the air with all its wonders.

Authors and Illustrators: Maria Rius, J. M. Parramon
Barron's, 1987. Hardcover: $5.95

Other books in the Habitat series:
Life Underground; Life on the Land; Life in the Sea

The Little Engine that Could

Value: Self-discipline

How many adults faced with a difficult task remember the story of *The Little Engine that Could*? "I think I can, I think I can," says the little engine, and she does! This story has inspired children and adults for two-thirds of a century. It is as good today as it was when I was a child. If you want to inspire your child just say, "I think I can. . . ." Then read this book as confirmation that we all can do it.

Author: Watty Piper, Illustrators: George and Doris Hauman
Putnam, 1930. Paperback: $5.95

Other books by this author:
Watty Piper's Trucks; Mother Goose: A Treasury of Best Loved Rhymes; Mother Goose Rhymes

Love You Forever

Values: All

When a baby is born parents say, "I'll love you forever, I'll like you for always. . . ." As the child grows through the "terrible twos," the pre-adolescent years, and then those challenging teen years, parents wonder if they can keep their pledge. This book always brings a tear to my eye, it is that touching. If you sometimes wonder if you can survive another day when "that child will drive me crazy," read this book. You may come away a better parent.

Author: Robert Munsch
Illustrator: Sheila McGraw
Firefly, 1986. Paperback: $4.95

Other books by this author:
I Have to Go!; The Fire Station; Angela's Airplane; The Boy in the Drawer; David's Father; Millicent and the Wind

Make Way for Ducklings

Honor: Caldecott Medal

Value: Generosity

When I meet adults who grew up with "Captain Kangaroo," this book is one of the works most often mentioned as a childhood treasure. I read it again and again on the program, and every time I received letters about how it was loved. Fifty years after Robert McCloskey first wrote this gem it remains immensely popular. Its greatness has been appreciated across generations. Oh, to visit Boston, the Public Garden, the Swan Boats, and to see the descendants of those ducklings, all eight of them, from Jack to Quack. This book is a gift to childhood.

Author and Illustrator: Robert McCloskey
Penguin, 1941. Paperback: $4.99

Other books by this author: *One Morning in Maine; Time of Wonder; Lentil*

On the Day You Were Born

The world is filled with miracles occurring each day, and none are greater than the miracle of a child's birth. When that miracle occurs, the world is bathed in other miracles, making life possible for the child on this cherished planet called earth. This lovely work weaves us all into the fabric of life and is a fitting welcome to each miraculous child arriving in our midst.

Author and Illustrator: Debra Frasier
Harcourt, 1991. Hardcover: $13.95

One fish, two fish, red fish, blue fish

Funny things are everywhere, especially in any book by Dr. Seuss. The genius of Ted Geisel is everywhere in this gift to children. Should I attempt to explain this book to you? Of course not! It is pure nonsense, and yet it makes the greatest sense. Giggle and enjoy!

Author and Illustrator: Dr. Seuss
Random House, 1960. Hardcover: $7.99

Other books by this author:
Hop on Pop; Fox in Socks; Green Eggs and Ham; Oh, the Places You'll Go!; Horton Hatches the Egg; Mr. Brown Can Moo! Can You?

One Smiling Grandma

A Caribbean Counting Book

This is a Caribbean counting book with colorful illustrations. It's suitable for a very young child and yet interesting to an older child. A lovely work.

Author: Ann Marie Linden, Illustrator: Lynne Russell
Penguin, 1992. Paperback: $4.99

Another book by this author:
Emerald Blue

The Real Mother Goose

It's difficult to believe that good old Mother Goose was so prolific. This volume contains almost three hundred rhymes, an encyclopedia of childhood from Little Bo Peep to When the Snow Is on the Ground. This is a joy for reading and a valuable reference work.

Illustrator: Blanche F. Wright
Scholastic, 1916. Hardcover: $7.95

Other illustrated versions of Mother Goose rhymes:
Mother Goose, illustrated by Tasha Tudor; *Mother Goose*, illustrated by Brian Wildsmith; *The Mother Goose Treasury*, illustrated by Raymond Briggs

2 to 6 Years

The Very Hungry Caterpillar

This book is just about perfect for young readers. The pages are sturdy, so young hands can manage the book with no worries. The pictures are very colorful, and the format is creative. On top of all that, this story is a lesson in the life-cycle of a caterpillar on the way to becoming a beautiful butterfly. This work is highly recommended.

Author and Illustrator: Eric Carle
Putnam, 1969. Boardbook: $7.95

Other books by this author:
Have You Seen My Cat?; The Grouchy Ladybug; Do You Want to Be My Friend?; Papa, Please Get the Moon for Me; A House for Hermit Crab; Walter the Baker

Books to Grow By

Books
for 3 ~ 6
Years
Old

3 to 6 Years

Arthur's Baby

Value: Trustworthiness

Parents are often challenged by sibling rivalry when a new baby arrives. In this tale, the parents give plenty of notice and time to get ready for the great event. Arthur's sister adopts a rather proprietary attitude toward the new baby, and insecure Arthur is left out of the action. Then one day the baby cries and cries and cries, and only Arthur seems to be a quieting influence on *his* baby. This book affords an opportunity for parents to prepare a sibling for a new arrival. The reading will lead to many questions for parents to answer.

Author and Illustrator: Marc Brown
Little, Brown & Co., 1987. Paperback: $4.95

Other books in this series:
Arthur's Birthday; Arthur's April Fool; Arthur's Eyes; Arthur's Valentine; Arthur's Nose; Arthur's Pet Business

The Bear's Toothache

Value: Generosity

The artwork in this book is outstanding, and the story is out of any child's imagination. A bear with a toothache is, well, it's unbearable! Try what you will, getting rid of that aching tooth is quite a feat. I would love to be there when the Tooth Fairy sees that tooth!

Author and Illustrator: David McPhail
Little, Brown & Co., 1972. Paperback: $5.95

Other books by this author:
*Emma's Vacation; Emma's Pet; First Flight;
Fix-It; Goldilocks and the Three Bears; The Three Little Pigs*

3 to 6 Years

The Berenstain Bears' Moving Day
Value: Generosity

The Berenstain Bears are among the most popular of children's book series. This may well be because they deal with challenges every child faces. When parents decide to leave one home for another, it is usually for a good reason. Children don't always understand those reasons, and they are among the most insecure of creatures—leaving behind the familiar can be a wrenching experience. Sure, we can pack our toys and books and favorite blanket, but what about friends? And what about my favorite room and my favorite rose bush? If you face a move, be sensitive to these childhood concerns. This book may help your child face the experience, and it may help you understand a child's concerns.

Authors and Illustrators: Stan and Jan Berenstain
Random House, 1981. Paperback: $2.50

Other books in this series: *The Berenstain Bears and the Week at Grandma's; The Berenstain Bears on the Moon; The Berenstain Bears and Too Much Birthday; The Berenstain Bears Forget Their Manners*

Other books by these authors: *Bears in the Night; Bears on Wheels; Inside, Outside, Upside Down*

The Big Snow

Honor: Caldecott Medal

Value: Generosity

This lovely book with beautiful pictures of animals is a primer on nature in the northern climes. It will cause children to think about the many animals with whom they share this earth, and it will be a special experience for urban children who may have never seen these animals in their natural habitat. The kindness shown by the humans in caring for the animals in a particularly difficult winter will be a model for children to emulate. I live in a northern country area, and each spring I rejoice when I see the deer and wild turkeys return to the meadow after a snowy winter. I would hope that every child could experience these feelings, and *The Big Snow* can be the first such experience.

Authors and Illustrators: Berta and Elmer Hader
Macmillan, 1948. Paperback: $4.95

Other books by these authors:
Reindeer Trail; Snow in the City

3 to 6 Years

Blueberries for Sal

Honor: Caldecott Honor

There is nothing tastier than blueberries freshly picked, but Sal's mother wants blueberries to "put up" for the wintertime. Mother Bear wants Little Bear to eat many blueberries to store up fat for wintertime. Robert McCloskey's charming story (remember *Make Way for Ducklings?*), will bring you straight to Blueberry Hill. This story is as tasty as blueberries.

Author and Illustrator: Robert McCloskey
Penguin, 1948. Paperback: $4.99

Other books by this author:
One Morning in Maine; Make Way for Ducklings; Time of Wonder

3 to 6 Years

Corduroy

Value: Fairness

This is one of Don Freeman's wonderful books, a touching story about a tiny bear on the store's toy shelf waiting for someone to take him home. Before this happens, Corduroy has some adventures in the closed and darkened department store. When a little girl, Lisa, buys him with money from her piggy bank, Corduroy knows he has found a friend.

Author and Illustrator: Don Freeman
Penguin, 1968. Paperback: $3.99

The sequel is:
A Pocket for Corduroy

Other books by this author:
Beady Bear; Chalk Box Story; Bearymore; Dandelion

The Elves and the Shoemaker

Value: Generosity

What cute elves they are, as pictured in this retelling of the famous fairy tale. Just as the elves returned every evening, so might you to revisit the shoemaker. The good feelings from this story are from the generosity exhibited by the elves and the shoemaker and his wife.

Retold by: Freya Littledale, Illustrator: Brinton Turkle
Scholastic, 1975. Paperback: $3.95

Other books by this author:
Peter and the North Wind; An Adaptation of Rip Van Winkle; The Magic Fish; The Farmer in the Soup

Frog and Toad Are Friends

Honor: Caldecott Honor

Value: Generosity

This book contains several stories and therefore can be read on different occasions, one story at a time. It is also a fine book for an older child who has some advanced reading skills. The stories are quite warm, and Frog and Toad display kindness and the generosity of true friendship for each other.

Author and Illustrator: Arnold Lobel
Harper, 1970. Paperback: $3.50

Other books in this series:
Frog and Toad All Year; Frog and Toad Together; Days with Frog and Toad

George and Martha

Value: Generosity

This is a terrific book about how friends should treat each other. It is five stories about the friendship of two hippos, George and Martha. Each story is short and delivers an easy message: friends should always tell each other the truth; privacy is important, even between friends; friends are cheerful and help others through difficult times. This is a primer on friendship. Who knows, perhaps reading this book will make your child a better friend, someone very nice with whom to share a day or evening.

Author and Illustrator: James Marshall
Houghton Mifflin, 1972. Paperback: $4.95

Other books in this series:
George and Martha Back in Town; George and Martha Encore; George and Martha One Fine Day; George and Martha Rise and Shine; George and Martha Tons of Fun; George and Martha Round and Round

Grandfather Twilight

Value: Generosity

This is a bedtime story in the classic sense. The soft illustrations add to the softness of the evening as twilight descends and the moon rises. I always wondered how this miracle occurred, and now I know.

Author and Illustrator: Barbara Berger
Philomel, 1984. Paperback: $5.95

Other books by this author:
When the Sun Rose; The Jewel Heart

Gregory, the Terrible Eater

Honor: Reading Rainbow

Value: Imagination

Having trouble getting a child to eat the right foods? Try a soup can, an auto tire, and dad's striped tie. His parents have a problem with Gregory, who happens to be a goat. A finicky eater will get the message in this story and digest it thoroughly. Yum, yum!

Author: Mitchell Sharmat
Illustrators: Jose Aruego and Ariane Dewey
Scholastic, 1980. Paperback: $3.95

Other books by this author:
Come Home, Wilma; Reddy Rattler and Easy Eagle; Sherman Is a Slowpoke

Harold and the Purple Crayon

Value: Imagination

If only we could all have a purple crayon like Harold's. But then, we do—it's called imagination. Harold's adventures with his crayon will delight children, or adults, for that matter. Adventure after adventure, and best of all, a nice night's sleep to end it all.

Author and Illustrator: Crockett Johnson
HarperCollins, 1955. Paperback: $3.95

Other books by this author:
Harold's ABC; Harold's Circus; Harold's Trip to the Sky; A Picture for Harold's Room

Harriet and Walt

Value: Generosity

A younger sibling can be a source of great frustration for any child, as Harriet knows all too well. Walt does get in the way of play, serious grown-up play, but when all is done, there's nothing quite like a nifty little brother ... or sister. Especially when they are asleep!

Author and Illustrator: Nancy Carlson
Carolrhoda, 1982. Paperback: $4.95

Other books in this series:
Harriet and the Garden; Harriet and the Roller Coaster;
Harriet's Halloween Candy; Harriet's Recital

Other books by this author:
I Like Me; Louanne Pig in Making the Team; Loudmouth George;
A Visit to Grandma's; The Big Race;
Arnie and the Skateboard Gang

Humphrey's Bear

Value: Generosity

A cherished toy can mean all things to a child. Humphrey's bear is hardly a toy—he is a friend, and what are friends for? To have adventures, to sail seas, to have pleasant dreams. Humphrey's father remembers those things, because once the bear took *him* on great adventures.

Author: Jan Wahl
Illustrator: William Joyce
Holt, 1987. Paperback: $5.95

Other books by this author:
Mrs. Owl and Mr. Pig; My Cat Ginger; The Adventures of Underwater Dog; Cabbage Moon; Carrot Nose; I Remember, Cried Grandma Pinky

I Need a Lunch Box

Value: Generosity

All children with older siblings look up to those siblings and yearn for the day when they, too, can have those "grown-up articles." A lunch box is often coveted by a younger sibling, and it becomes a symbol of reaching a more mature age. In this charmer, a young child dreams of the day when he will possess a lunch box like his sister Doris. Dreams are made to be fulfilled, and this one is no exception.

Author: Jeanette Caines, Illustrator: Pat Cummings
HarperCollins, 1988. Paperback: $4.95

Other books by this author:
Abby; Just Us Women; Daddy; Chilly Stomach; Window Wishing

ion Dancer
Ernie Wan's Chinese New Year

Honor: Reading Rainbow

Value: Self-discipline

Gung-Hey-Fat-Choy, Happy Chinese New Year! This is the marvelous story of a young boy named Ernie Wan and his first experience as a lion dancer at the Chinese New Year. The action, and it is action, is photographed in color in New York's Chinatown. You will feel the thrill of being a part of this wonderful feast. The back of the book contains a Chinese horoscope. Find the year of your birth and read the text. My birth-year tells me I am "nice to be around and many people trust me." Trust me, this is a terrific book for all ages.

Authors: Kate Waters and Madeline Slovenz-Low
Photography: Martha Cooper
Scholastic, 1990. Paperback: $3.95

Another book by these authors:
The Story of the White House

Little Bear

Value: Generosity

This wonderful story of a little bear and his loving mother is one that all young children can understand. The adventures of little bear are the same sort of dreams and frolics that any small child might have. The illustrations, done early in Maurice Sendak's career, are a delight.

Author: Else Holmelund Minarik
Illustrator: Maurice Sendak
HarperCollins, 1957. Paperback: $3.50

Other books by this author:
*Little Bear's Friend; Little Bear's Visit; A Kiss for Little Bear;
Am I Beautiful?; No Fighting, No Biting*

3 to 6 Years

The Little House

Honor: Caldecott Medal

Value: Generosity

Once again, Virginia Lee Burton spins a tale children will love. Most children resist change, and in that way, they are like the little house. The greatest changes occur all about the little house as the city grows up around it. It isn't a good time for the little house, but have no fear, there is a happy ending.

Author and Illustrator: Virginia Lee Burton
Houghton, 1942. Paperback: $4.95

Other books by this author:
Katy and the Big Snow; Mike Mulligan and His Steam Shovel;
Choo Choo: The Story of a Little Engine Who Ran Away;
Maybelle, the Cable Car

The Little Red Hen An Old Story

Value: Self-discipline

This is a retelling of the classic story of all the animals who shy away from the work of baking bread but who are all prepared to eat the tasty loaf when it pops from the oven. A child needs to learn the relationship between the rewards in life and old-fashioned hard work. This tale will make that point.

Illustrator: Margot Zemach
Farrar, Straus, 1983. Paperback: $4.95

Other books by this author:
*The Three Little Pigs; The Three Wishes; It Could Always Be Worse;
The Fisherman and His Wife; Three Sillies;
The Three Wishes: An Old Story*

Millions of Cats

Honor: Newbery Honor

Value: Generosity

This classic was written about the time I was born, and that is a very long time ago. This tale of millions of cats has enchanted millions of children—and for good reason. Read it and try to decide who, among millions of cats, is prettiest of all. Meow!

Author and Illustrator: Wanda Gág
Putnam, 1928. Paperback: $4.95

Other books by this author:
*The ABC Bunny; Gone Is Gone; Wanda Gág's: Six Swans;
Snow White and the Seven Dwarfs; The Funny Thing;
Wanda Gág's: The Earth Gnome;
Nothing at All*

Noah's Ark

Honor: Caldecott Medal

The Biblical story of the flood is well told by a brief poem in the book's opening pages. The rest of the book is simply illustrations, letting parents and children tell the story together. The wonderful details show you new things each time you look. Try to count the animals!

Retold and illustrated by: Peter Spier
Dell, 1977. Paperback: $4.99

Other books by this author:
Fast - Slow, High - Low; Gobble, Growl, Grunt; Peter Spier's Circus!; Peter Spier's Rain

Noisy Nora

Value: Fairness

Nora is a noisy little mouse, trying to get her parents' attention, but they're all tied up with Nora's brother and sister. Fed up with waiting, Nora pretends to leave—and when all is quiet, she's missed by her family.

Author and Illustrator: Rosemary Wells
Penguin, 1973. Paperback: $3.99

Other books by this author:
Hazel's Amazing Mother; Max's Dragon Shirt; Max's First Word; Shy Charles; Stanley and Rhoda

The Quilt Story

What could be as warm as a fine quilt? Well, this story about a quilt will warm you as you travel through the generations, following a quilt, the little girls who love it, and the places the quilt helps make feel like home.

Author: Tony Johnston
Illustrator: Tomie dePaola
Putnam, 1985. Paperback: $5.95

Other books by this author:
Grandpa's Song; The Badger and the Magic Fan: A Japanese Folktale; The Witch's Hat; The Soup Bone; The Vanishing Pumpkin

Rosie's Walk

If you think you are such a wise fox, don't be dumb enough to chase Rosie the hen as she takes a walk. Children will giggle at all that happens to the fox when he follows Rosie on her quiet walk.

Author and Illustrator: Pat Hutchins
Macmillan, 1968. Paperback: $4.95

Other books by this author:
Good-Night, Owl!;
What Game Shall We Play?;
Changes, Changes;
Where's the Baby?

3 to 6 Years

The Snowy Day

Honor: Caldecott Medal

Value: Imagination

This charmer by Ezra Jack Keats was always one of my favorites. Peter, a young boy, enjoys the fun and magic of a new-fallen snow. Try building a snowman, try making angels in the snow, and at nighttime, try to figure out what happened to that snowball you stuffed in your pocket. A delight!

Author and Illustrator: Ezra Jack Keats
Puffin, 1962. Paperback: $4.99

Other books by this author:
Apt. 3, Pet Show!; Whistle for Willie; Regards to the Man in the Moon; Dreams; Peter's Chair

The Three Bears

Value: Fairness

Paul Galdone retells this favorite story of childhood, and his illustrations are quite humorous. Even if you don't care for porridge, you will find this book very tasty.

Author and Illustrator: Paul Galdone
Houghton Mifflin, 1972. Paperback: $5.95

Other books by this author:
The Gingerbread Boy; The Three Sillies; The Princess and the Pea; The Hare and the Tortoise; Cinderella; The Elves and the Shoemaker

The Three Little Pigs

Value: Self-discipline

I'll tell you, between the three pigs and Red Riding Hood, this wolf is getting a very bad reputation. He's back from Grandma's house and in hot pursuit of three delicious little pigs. If you want to stop this wolf in his tracks, better build a house of stone, or aluminum siding, or steel, or, perhaps, some bricks!

Retold by: Jennifer Greenway, Illustrator: Debbie Dieneman
Ariel, 1991. Paperback: $6.95

Other books by this author:
Goldilocks and the Three Bears; Jack and the Beanstalk; The Three Billy-Goats Gruff

3 to 6 Years

The Tortoise and the Hare
An Aesop Fable

Value: Self-discipline

This Aesop fable is the great lesson about diligence and stick-to-it-tiveness. The race, or the reward, is not always to the fastest or the brightest. Hard work usually wins out. These aren't bad lessons for a child to learn early in life. This version by Janet Stevens features some very humorous illustrations.

Aesop's fable illustrated by: Janet Stevens
Holiday, 1984. Hardcover: $14.95

Other stories by Aesop:
The City Mouse and the Country Mouse; The Lion and the Mouse; Little Red Riding Hood; The Miller, His Son, and Their Donkey

The Twins, Two by Two

Just as in their bedtime story about the Ark, twins Minnie and Max go up to bed two by two. Pretending to be two monkeys, two bears, or two elephants is a fun bedtime game to play.

Authors and Illustrators: Catherine and Laurence Anholt
Candlewick Press, 1992. Paperback: $4.99

Other books by these authors:
*All about You; What I Like; Bear and Baby; Come Back, Jack!;
Here Come the Babies; Kids*

Will I Have a Friend?

Value: Generosity

This is a fine book to read to a youngster who is close to starting school or day care. Making friends in such a place is a concern for children, though they may not talk about it. After reading this book, you can discuss making friends, especially how important it is to reach out to other children.

Author: Miriam Cohen, Illustrator: Lillian Hoban
Macmillan, 1967. Paperback: $3.95

Other books by this author:
No Good in Art?; So What?; Jim's Dog Muffins; Jim Meets the Thing; Best Friends; Don't Eat Too Much Turkey; It's George!

William's Doll

This book was always a favorite of mine. In the two decades since it first appeared, the need to teach nurturing to boys and young men has become greater because of changes in family structure. William wants to nurture and that . . . well, that worries some people who think that stuff is for sissies. William, they think, ought to be playing trains and basketball—which he does, by the way, and does very well. We get so hung up on gender that we can do damage to young children. Nurturing is a masculine as well as a feminine skill. We need strong fathers as well as strong mothers in our society, and our culture ought to assign strong, masculine attributes to nurturing. This book is a tribute to strong, nurturing fathers, and being a strong, nurturing father is about as masculine as you can get.

Author: Charlotte Zolotow, Illustrator: William Pene Du Bois
HarperCollins, 1972. Paperback: $4.95

Other books by this author:
Do You Know What I'll Do?; But Not Billy; This Quiet Lady; Something Is Going to Happen

Books for 3~8 Years Old

Abuela's Weave

Values: Self-discipline / Generosity

Our children are enriched when exposed to children in different cultures, and this story is rich in the culture of Guatemala, Central America. We are introduced to the family "compound," where young Esperanza's mother feeds the pigs and chickens while Esperanza's brothers are in the fields with crops of corn, beans, and coffee. Esperanza learns to weave from her Grandmother Abuela, and she also learns patience, an important virtue to display to children. Esperanza also fears that people will make fun of her grandmother, who has a facial birthmark. Any child will sympathize with this granddaughter and come to know that teasing anyone can be very cruel. We follow Esperanza as she makes the long trip on foot and by bus to the marketplace, where at first she is not well received and then successfully sells her wares. The trip home by bus is a warm scene rich in the love displayed across generations.

Author: Omar S. Castaneda, Illustrator: Enrique O. Sanchez
Lee & Low Books, 1993. Paperback: $5.95.

All Those Secrets of the World

Honor: Reading Rainbow

This poignant book was published in the nineties but has echoes carrying across generations. The moving text and lovely watercolors brought me to my childhood and the questions I asked in those tender, vulnerable years. The book is filled with love and the childhood pain of missing someone gone far away. The reunion, the butterfly kisses, and the whispering sycamores help to reveal so many of the great secrets that all children wonder about.

Author: Jane Yolen, Illustrator: Leslie Baker
Little, Brown, & Co, 1991. Paperback: $4.95.

Other books by this author:
Mouse's Birthday; Owl Moon; Piggins; Picnic with Piggins; Sky Dogs; Welcome to the Green House; Ring of Earth

3 to 8 Years

Annie and the Wild Animals

Value: Self-discipline

Annie lives in a small cottage in the deep, deep woods. The winter snows make it a place that can be lonely, except that Annie has a special friend, her cat Taffy. One day Taffy disappears into the snows. Annie, in search of a new pet, bakes corn cakes and leaves them at the edge of the woods. Many animals come and they eat many corn cakes, but none is furry and friendly, none can be tamed as a pet. In springtime, with the snows gone, Annie longs for the friend she has so missed—when out of the woods comes Taffy and three cuddly kittens. Annie will be lonely no more. This story is much like a fairy tale and, like good fairy tales, has a warm and fuzzy ending.

Author and Illustrator: Jan Brett
Houghton, 1985. Paperback: $4.95

Other books by this author:
The Mitten; Trouble with Trolls; The Wild Christmas Reindeer; Berlioz the Bear; First Dog

Bringing the Rain to Kapiti Plain

Honor: Reading Rainbow

Value: Self-discipline

Everyone and everything living on this earth depends on rain to grow the grass and crops, to sustain life. This charming story is based on folklore from Kenya. It is told in a rhythm that will fascinate a child. The pictures capture the flavor of life on the African plain. The story will allow a reader to talk with a child about rain and our need for it. Rainy days are often a disappointment to children, but if they can appreciate the benefits, perhaps rain will become a joy.

Retold by: Verna Aardema, Illustrator: Beatriz Vidal
Penguin, 1981. Paperback: $4.99.

Other books by this author:
The Vingananee and the Tree Toad; Traveling to Tondo: A Tale of the Nkundo of Zaire; Anansi Finds a Fool; Princess Gorilla and a New Kind of Water

3 to 8 Years

Caps for Sale

Honor: Reading Rainbow

Value: Imagination

This is one of my favorites. I would read this book on "Captain Kangaroo" regularly, and to this day I have people tell me what a favorite story it was for them. Perhaps you remember the story from your youth. Its continued popularity demonstrates the fun that children find across generations. Monkey see, monkey do, is what this is all about, and children delight in the last few pages. You may read this book to a child today with the assurance that *they* will be reading it to their children.

Author and Illustrator: Esphyr Slobodkina
HarperCollins, 1940. Paperback: $3.95.

Other books by this author:
The Little Dinghy; Pezzo the Peddler and the Thirteen Thieves;
The Wonderful Feast

3 to 8 Years

Curious George

Value: Imagination

This is the first in the Curious George series of adventures, and it's a good one. A child will feel for George, the curious monkey, because most children are also curious. A child, without our vast adult experience, is on a voyage of discovery, and there is so much to learn, so much to tweak our curiosity. George is captured in Africa because of his curiosity, falls in the big ocean because of his curiosity, telephones the fire department because of his curiosity. This book is worth many giggles. A reader might talk to a child about healthy curiosity and when to restrain curiosity just a bit. This is a lesson that George never learns in this or in the subsequent delightful adventures.

Author and Illustrator: H. A. Rey
Houghton Mifflin, 1941. Paperback: $4.95.

Other books in this series: *Curious George Flies a Kite; Curious George Learns the Alphabet; Curious George Rides a Bike; Curious George Takes a Job; Curious George Goes to the Hospital; Curious George Goes Fishing*

3 to 8 Years

Fathers, Mothers, Sisters, Brothers A Collection of Family Poems

Honor: Reading Rainbow

All children are curious about their family and curious about other families. This collection of poems—funny poems, nice poems, warm poems—encompasses every conceivable family and family member. So many family experiences are covered here! This big, happy family will extend the world of any child to our extended family.

Author: Mary Ann Hoberman
Illustrator: Marylin Hafner
Penguin, 1991. Paperback: $4.99

Other books by this author: *A House Is a House for Me; Bugs: Poems; The Cozy Book; A Fine Fat Pig and Other Animal Poems; I Like Old Clothes*

Frederick

Honor: Caldecott Honor

Value: Imagination

Many parents mistakenly think of imagination as frivolous and urge young children to get down to the "reality of life." Yet imagination is critical in any profession, medicine, the law, business. A well-developed imagination gets us through the stark reality of daily life. A wise mouse, Frederick, teaches his siblings how to store up images and use imagination during the harsh days of a cruel winter. Help your children to use imagination to be more productive but also to find greater happiness. Little Frederick will give you some helpful hints on how to accomplish this critical goal.

Author and Illustrator: Leo Lionni
Knopf, 1967. Paperback: $4.99.

Other books by this author:
Mr. McMouse; Nicolas, Where Have You Been?; Frederick's Fables; Swimmy; A Busy Year; The Biggest House in the World; Inch by Inch; It's Mine

The Grouchy Ladybug

Value: Fairness

We have all met people much like the grouchy lady-bug. Children will delight as the adventures of this grouchy lady grow bigger and BIGGER! We can all learn the lessons of not being cantankerous, sharing with others, and enjoying life.

Author and Illustrator: Eric Carle
HarperCollins, 1977. Paperback: $5.95

Other books by this author: *The Very Busy Spider; The Mixed-Up Chameleon; The Very Quiet Cricket; The Very Hungry Caterpillar*

3 to 8 Years

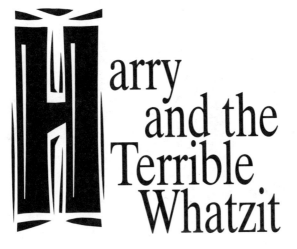

Harry and the Terrible Whatzit

Value: Courage

It is a terrible whatzit until Harry learns its secret, a secret every child must learn. If you have a child who is afraid of the monsters under the bed and in the dark corner—and what child is not—this is a good story. It deals with the whatzits and monsters and enables a child to do the same.

Author and Illustrator: Dick Gackenbach
Houghton Mifflin, 1977. Paperback: $5.95.

Other books by this author:
A Bag Full of Pups; Hound and Bear; Poppy the Panda; Mighty Tree; Claude the Dog; Claude and Pepper

Harry the Dirty Dog

Has anyone seen Harry? This was always one of my favorite reads on "Captain Kangaroo." Most children enjoy the daily bath, but if you have a reluctant bather, this book is for them. The adventures of Harry are a delight, and when he is so dirty that not even his loving family recognizes him, well, it's time for this old dog to learn some tricks. A great story.

Author: Gene Zion
Illustrator: Margaret Bloy Graham
HarperCollins, 1956. Paperback: $4.95

Other books by this author:
Harry Comes Home; Harry by the Sea; Harry and the Lady Next Door; No Roses for Harry; Hide and Seek Day; Dear Garbage Man; Sugar Mouse Cake

Hot-Air Henry

Honor: Reading Rainbow

One of the most exciting adventures is a ride in a hot-air balloon. This story takes a child on such a trip with Hot-Air Henry, an adventuresome feline. The pictures are beautiful and the technical aspects of ballooning are accurate. This is a great adventure. As the old expression says, "Curiosity flew the cat!"

Author: Mary Calhoun
Illustrator: Erick Ingraham
William Morrow, 1981. Paperback: $4.95.

Other books by this author:
Cross-Country Cat; High-Wire Henry; While I Sleep; Wobble the Witch Cat

3 to 8 Years

Lyle, Lyle Crocodile

If you put on your skates and glide across the ice, don't be surprised to see Lyle Crocodile sharing the fun with you. This nifty book is about a very unusual crocodile who teaches some austere humans all about the art of being gentle and kind.

Author and Illustrator: Bernard Waber
Houghton, 1965. Paperback: $5.95.

Other books by this author:
Lyle and the Birthday Party; Lyle Finds His Mother;
Ira Sleeps Over; Ira Says Goodbye;
An Anteater Named Arthur

Mike Mulligan and His Steam Shovel

Value: Self-discipline

Another great book, both story and pictures, from Virginia Lee Burton. Of all the stories read on "Captain Kangaroo," this is at the top of the popularity list. Adults always seem to recall the Captain reading this book to them. The surprise ending, the solution to the problem, is a delight. Share this wonder with any child, and you will give a cherished lifetime memory.

Author and Illustrator: Virginia Lee Burton
Houghton, 1939. Paperback: $4.95.

Other books by this author:
Katy and the Big Snow; The Little House; Maybelle, the Cable Car; Choo Choo: The Story of a Little Engine Who Ran Away

3 to 8 Years

Miss Rumphius

Value: Generosity

What a lovely gift to give a child—the notion of someday making the world more beautiful. If every child everywhere grew to fulfill that quest, what a beautiful world we would inhabit. This is a lovely story, and the pictures are perfect.

Author and Illustrator: Barbara Cooney
Penguin, 1982. Paperback: $4.99

Other books by this author:
Chanticleer and the Fox (retold); Hattie and the Wild Waves:
A Story from Brooklyn; The Little Juggler

3 to 8 Years

Mr. Rabbit and the Lovely Present

Honor: Caldecott Honor

Value: Generosity

What makes a special present for someone you love? Charlotte Zolotow's text is charming, and the pictures by Maurice Sendak make it all happen. This book is a lovely present for any child.

Author: Charlotte Zolotow
Illustrator: Maurice Sendak
HarperCollins, 1962. Paperback: $4.50.

Other books by this author:
*The Seashore Book; The Bunny Who Found Easter;
The Beautiful Christmas Tree; I Like to Be Little*

3 to 8 Years

The Mitten

This Ukrainian folktale is beautifully told and beautifully illustrated. Some of the woodland creatures found in Ukraine come together in a moment of sharing, until the last tiny creature becomes one too many. This is a lovely story.

Editor/Author: Alvin Tresselt
Illustrator: Yaroslava Mills
Morrow, 1964. Paperback: $4.95

Other books by this author:
Sun Up; Wake Up, City!; Wake Up, Farm!;
The Rabbit Story

3 to 8 Years

Nine Days to Christmas

Honor: Caldecott Medal

This story is about a little Mexican girl and her first posada, a special Christmas party complete with a piñata. It is a sensitive tale of Mexican culture as well. Many families from this culture share our country with us, and this book introduces children to that land and its children. It is a lovely book by one of my favorite authors, Marie Hall Ets.

Authors: Marie Hall Ets and Aurora Labastida
Illustrator: Marie Hall Ets
Penguin, 1959. Paperback: $4.99.

Other books by these authors:
Gilberto and the Wind; In the Forest; Just Me; Play with Me

Norman the Doorman

Value: Trustworthiness

Don Freeman is one of my favorite children's authors, and his *Norman the Doorman* is wonderful. This is a mouse with style as well as courage— not to mention great artistic talents. This is a book you will enjoy while reading it to your young person.

Author and Illustrator: Don Freeman
Penguin, 1959. Paperback: $4.99

Other books by this author:
Beady Bear; Bearymore; Dandelion; The Chalk Box Story; A Rainbow of My Own

Old Turtle

Values: All

This is an awesome book. At a time ages ago, when animals could talk to each other, they carried on a debate to describe God. The debate becomes a noisy animal until Old Turtle says "Stop!" and predicts a new species on earth, a species of people to be like God. But when the people come, they forget who they are. They argue and hurt each other and hurt the earth, until another voice speaks with wisdom, reminding people of who they are and of the kindness needed by a dying earth. It does not matter what your theological beliefs may be. This powerful book is an advocate for peace on earth and kindness to the earth. The text is wonderful and the watercolors are perfect. This book is a winner. It may influence young attitudes for a lifetime and is sure to reach your heart.

Author: Douglas Wood, Illustrator: Cheng-Khee Chee
Pfeifer Hamilton, 1992. Hardcover: $17.95

Pancakes for Breakfast

Value: Self-discipline

Tomie dePaola keeps coming up with enchantment.
There are few words in this story, so the youngest child
can follow along. I even got hungry in the middle pages!

Author and Illustrator: Tomie dePaola
Harcourt, 1978. Paperback: $4.95

Other books by this author:
Andy; That's My Name; Charlie Needs a Cloak; Haircuts for the Woolseys;
Little Grunt and the Big Egg: A Prehistoric Fairy Tale;
Nana Upstairs and Nana Downstairs

Peter and the Wolf

Value: Courage

The illustrations in this book are simply magnificent, capturing the Russian countryside, the peasants, and most of all the nasty wolf. This is a fine version of the Prokofiev tale and, if I might suggest, a wonderful stepping stone to Sergei Prokofiev's musical version of "Peter and the Wolf." I know classical music is not a favorite with many young people these days, but for the sake of their cultural literacy they ought to be exposed to it. The musical Peter is a wonderful first exposure, and with this book in hand while listening, the experience should be most rewarding.

Author: Sergei Prokofiev (translated by Maria Carlson)
Illustrator: Charles Mikolaycak
Penguin, 1982. Paperback: $5.99

3 to 8 Years

The Polar Express

Honor: Caldecott Medal

Value: Generosity

This is a great story and should be a Christmas classic. The illustrations are fabulous. The story is about believing the dreams of childhood. The older we grow, the less we believe, unless you are one of those rare adults who has not lost childhood to the years. Rediscover childhood in this book.

Author and Illustrator: Chris Van Allsburg
Houghton Mifflin, 1985. Hardcover: $17.95

Other books by this author:
Just a Dream; The Stranger; Two Bad Ants; The Widow's Broom; The Wreck of the Zephyr; Jumanji; The Garden Book of Abdul Gasazi; Ben's Dream

3 to 8 Years

Red Riding Hood

Value: Trustworthiness

This version of the classic is in verse and a tasty telling it is. Almost as tasty as the baked goodies in that little girl's basket. I'd offer you one but they are promised to Grandma.

Retold by: Beatrice Schenk de Regniers
Illustrator: Edward Gorey
Macmillan, 1972. Paperback: $4.95

Other books by this author:
Jack and the Beanstalk; Jack the Giant Killer; May I Bring a Friend?; Shadow Book; Waiting for Mama

The Story about Ping

How many times have I read *Ping* on television? I cannot tell you, it has been that many. *Ping* never loses its charm, and today's children will enjoy it as much as previous generations. Share it with a child you love.

Author: Marjorie Flack
Illustrator: Kurt Wiese
Puffin, 1933. Paperback: $4.99

Other books by this author:
Angus and the Cat; Angus and the Ducks; Ask Mr. Bear; Angus Lost

Summer Story

Value: Generosity

This is a lovely story of romance from Great Britain, and very charming it is. The illustration detail is fascinating. This story has a distinctly British air to it, so civilized, so . . . well, so very polite. It seems even the country mice in Britain are civil creatures.

Author and Illustrator: Jill Barklem
Putnam, 1980. Hardcover: $10.95

Other books in this series:
Autumn Story; Winter Story; Spring Story

Other books by this author:
Sea Story; The Secret Staircase

The Tale of Peter Rabbit

Value: Trustworthiness

For almost a century, children throughout the world have enjoyed Beatrix Potter's tales. They are a legacy of childhood and should be enjoyed by every child everywhere. Don't let your child be the exception to this great experience.

Author and Illustrator: Beatrix Potter
Penguin, 1902. Hardcover: $5.95

Other books in this series:
The Tale of Jeremy Fisher; The Tale of Mrs. Tittlemouse and Other Mouse Stories; Hill Top Tales; Four Original Peter Rabbit Stories; The Complete Adventures of Tom Kitten; Benjamin Bunny; Jemima Puddle-Duck; The Tale of Johnny Town-Mouse

Books for 4~8 Years Old

4 to 8 Years

Amazing Grace

Honor: Reading Rainbow

Values: Courage / Self-discipline / Imagination

As soon as you see the cover you will fall in love with Grace. She is a girl in love with stories, stories from books read to her, stories from movies, stories she makes up, or stories from Nana's memory. (What a kind face Nana shows us in telling a story to Grace!) Grace is a young lady with imagination with a capital "I," and when her classmates tell her she cannot play Peter Pan in the class play, watch out. Don't mess with Grace, baby, she is one determined young lady. All questions are settled after the auditions, and her classmates begin to call her "fantastic." What she is, quite simply, is Amazing Grace. The pictures are beautiful.

Author: Mary Hoffman, Illustrator: Caroline Binch
Penguin, 1991. Hardcover: $14.99

Other books by this author:
Boundless Grace; My Grandma Has Black Hair; Nancy No-Size; Henry's Baby

4 to 8 Years

Amelia's Fantastic Flight

Value: Imagination

Amelia loves airplanes, so she builds one. Just as simple as that! When you fly on imagination, the ordinary logistics of life don't get in the way. This is a super geography lesson, which should bring happiness to all those adults who feel children don't know where in the world they are. Fly with Amelia, you'll like it! And you'll be home in time for dinner and a good bedtime story.

Author and Illustrator: Rose Bursik
Holt, 1992. Paperback: $5.95

Another book by this author:
Zoe's Sheep

4 to 8 Years

Anansi the Spider
A Tale from the Ashanti

Honor: Caldecott Honor

Values: All

This book is a beautiful tale from the Ashanti of West Africa. Anansi the spider has six sons, six good sons. When Anansi falls into trouble, he is rescued by all his sons, each using his special talent. It is a delightful story with a special conclusion from a rich folklore. You will never look at the moon in the same way again.

Author and Illustrator: Gerald McDermott
Holt, 1972. Paperback: $5.95

Other books by this author:
*Arrow to the Sun; Daniel O'Rourke:
An Irish Tale; Zomo the Rabbit:
A Trickster Tale from West Africa; Raven:
A Trickster Tale from the Pacific Northwest;
Sunflight*

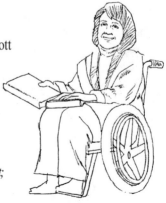

4 to 8 Years

Bea and Mr. Jones

Honor: Reading Rainbow

Value: Imagination

The grass is always greener in someone else's back yard, and after this book I believe it. Does a child ever wonder what a parent does at work? Does a child ever tire of kindergarten? The answer to both questions is "yes," and to find out what to do about it, ask either Bea or her father, Mr. Jones.

Author and Illustrator: Amy Schwartz
Macmillan, 1982. Paperback: $3.95

Other books by this author:
Begin at the Beginning; Annabelle Swift, Kindergartner; Oma and Bobo; Yossel Zessel and the Wisdom of Chelm; Camper of the Week; A Teeny, Tiny Baby

Bedtime for Frances

Value: Fairness

Often the most frustrating time of a day for a parent is bedtime, which a child will find any excuse to avoid. Children can be so *very* creative in thinking up reasons for not going off to sleep. A child is a very social person, and the company of parents is something they do not want to end by ending the day. A child can display genuine fears about a darkened room where monsters seem real in a young mind. However, most parents understand the need to establish bedtime routines early in childhood. Bedtime stories are a welcome compromise for the child who wants just a bit more of mommy and daddy before falling off to sleep. *Bedtime for Frances* is a reassuring book for children and parents, and it models behavior for frustrated parents to follow.

Author: Russell Hoban, Illustrator: Garth Williams
HarperCollins, 1960. Paperback: $4.95

Other books by this author: *A Bargain for Frances; A Baby Sister for Frances; Bread and Jam for Frances; Best Friends for Frances; A Birthday for Frances; Monsters; Arthur's New Power*

Begin at the Beginning

Honor: Reading Rainbow

Professional writers call it "writer's block." Actors, physicians, lawyers, everyone experiences it. Before any creation—a painting, a story, a medical procedure—we have to mull it over, and we have to begin at the beginning. Sara is a very talented young lady who discovers a simple truth. With all her talent and imagination, she must begin at the beginning before she can deal with the universe. Organizing thought processes is something any child must learn on the way to maturity. Sara's experience will be a help in developing this process in a child. Please don't forget, when you read the book, begin at the beginning!

Author and Illustrator: Amy Schwartz
HarperCollins, 1983. Paperback: $3.95

Other books by this author:
Bea and Mr. Jones; Camper of the Week; Annabelle Swift, Kindergartner; Oma and Bobo; Yossel Zissel and the Wisdom of Chelm

Ben's Trumpet

Honor: Caldecott Honor

Values: Generosity / Imagination

What hat child has not pretended to play a musical instrument, an instrument purely in his or her imagination? Ben plays and plays and plays, until one day, he gets his big break as a jazz trumpeter puts a real horn in Ben's hands and begins to teach the art. Ben is probably making a compact disc as we read about his beginnings. It all begins with an active imagination.

Author and Illustrator: Rachel Isadora
Mulberry, 1979. Paperback: $4.95

Other books by this author:
At the Crossroads; Over the Green Hills; Lili at the Ballet;
Max; My Ballet Class; Swan Lake

The Bicycle Man

Honor: Reading Rainbow

Value: Generosity

This is a sweet story about the initial experience of Japanese school children with American soldiers shortly after the end of World War II. The meeting of the two cultures, at first timorous, then warm, then enthusiastic, makes for a gentle story. The world has changed in the fifty years since the time of this story, but what has not changed is the need for different cultures to display respect and to share a world. Children will be impressed with the games the Japanese school children play, the races, tug of war, piggyback. They could take place on a school playground in Indiana or Texas.

Author and Illustrator: Allen Say
Houghton Mifflin, 1982. Paperback: $5.95

Other books by this author:
Tree of Cranes; River Dream; The Lost Lake; Grandfather's Journey

4 to 8 Years

The Big Orange Splot

Value: Imagination

From early childhood, it is difficult for a child to be different, to like different foods, to play different games. Peer pressure to be the same as everyone else is intense in childhood. This lovely story tells the wonderful tale of things that happened on a "neat street." Perhaps being yourself, even if that is different, is not so bad after all.

Author and Illustrator: Daniel Pinkwater
Scholastic, 1977. Paperback: $3.95

Other books by this author:
Aunt Lulu; Roger's Umbrella; The Phantom of the Lunch Wagon;
Guys from Space; Magic Camera; Pickle Creature; Tooth-gnasher superflash

4 to 8 Years

A Chair for My Mother

Honors: Caldecott Honor / Reading Rainbow

Value: Generosity

Many books for children deal with wonderful worlds of imagination. This one deals with reality in a most heartwarming way. Rosa and her hard-working mother and her grandmother share the joys and the disappointments of daily life. Rosa is determined to buy a comfortable chair for her mother to rest in upon returning from work. She saves coin after coin—what perseverance. She displays admirable patience, a wonderful virtue in a world where instant gratification is encouraged by the world surrounding us. This book is made for children living in single-parent families and fosters understanding on the part of all children.

Author and Illustrator: Vera B. Williams
William Morrow, 1982. Paperback: $4.95

Other books by this author: *Something Special for Me; Music, Music for Everyone; Three Days on a River in a Red Canoe*

4 to 8 Years

The Children's Aesop
Selected Fables

Values: All

If morals were gold—and as character traits they may be as valuable—this retelling of Aesop's fables by Stephanie Calmenson is a gold mine. There are as many character-building stories here as a parent could want. The twenty-eight in this collection include the Hare and the Tortoise, the Shepherd Boy and the Wolf, and the Goose Who Laid the Golden Eggs. Take this book, read it to a child, one or two fables at a time, and have some conversation about each one. It's called character building. A child will never forget these fables. You didn't!

Retold by: Stephanie Calmenson
Illustrator: Robert Byrd Boyds
Mills Press, 1988. Hardcover: $14.95

Other books by this author:
Roller Skates!; Wanted: Warm, Furry Friend; The Principal's New Clothes; Dinner at the Panda Palace; Hotter than a Hotdog

Christopher Robin Leads an Expotition

Value: Imagination

On "Captain Kangaroo," we always received a great response when we told the tale of Christopher Robin going to the Palace with Alice to watch the changing of the guard. It is a wonderful piece of material, as are all A. A. Milne stories about Christopher Robin. They present such a delightful set of characters, Pooh and Roo, Piglet and Eeyore. The twisting of language and the nonsense make so much . . . well, so much *sense* in the world of children. Rediscover your youth as you read this Christopher Robin tale to a giggling child.

Author: A. A. Milne, Illustrator: Ernest H. Shepard
Dutton Children's Books, 1926. Paperback: $4.99

Other books by this author: *The House at Pooh Corner; Now We Are Six; The Pooh Story Book; Pooh's Bedtime Book; When We Were Very Young*

Cinderella

Honor: Caldecott Medal

Value: Fairness

This telling of a great fable by Marcia Brown is very stylish and does justice to the original Charles Perrault tale. The language is lovely and embellishes a simple story. Everyone knows what happens when the slipper is a perfect fit for Cinderella's foot. Of course, she goes to the palace to live and the prince marries her three days later. (He must have known someone in the marriage license bureau who waived the usual waiting period.) A child will enjoy the story as never before because the language and the pictures are so lovely. Hurry to read this one before the clock strikes midnight!

Translated and illustrated by: Marcia Brown
Macmillan, 1954. Paperback: $4.95

Other books by this author: *Stone Soup; Dick Whittington and His Cat; Once a Mouse: A Fable Cut in Wood*

Dawn

Value: Generosity

Most American children live in urban or suburban settings. It is very difficult to bring such children into contact with our earth on any regular basis. This enchanting book, with its vibrant pictures, suggests the experience we should feel in the miracle of life on earth. Our Mother Earth embraces us in this work.

Author and Illustrator: Uri Shulevitz
Farrar, 1974. Paperback: $5.95

Other books by this author:
The Treasure; One Monday Morning; Rain Rain Rivers

Doctor De Soto

Honor: Newbery Honor

Value: Courage

The doctor is a dentist and also a mouse, so imagine
his quandary when faced with a mouse's arch enemy—
a red fox, a fox with a toothache. Generous of nature,
as is his wife, Doctor De Soto extracts the tooth and
promises a new tooth ready the next day. My favorite
line is from the fox on his way home, wondering if it
would be "shabby of him" to eat the mice after tomorrow's visit. The thought also occurs to the De Sotos, and
if you want to know how to outfox a fox, read this story.
Doctor De Soto's dentistry is unorthodox, but his
instincts for survival are as sharp as a polished bicuspid.

Author and Illustrator: William Steig
Farrar, 1982. Paperback: $4.95

Other books by this author: *Dr. De Soto Goes to Africa; Brave Irene; Amos
and Boris; Farmer Palmer's Wagon Ride; Sylvester and the Magic Pebble*

The Emperor's New Clothes

Value: Fairness

The great storyteller Hans Christian Andersen first fitted us for this story, and now it is retold with absolutely charming and humorous illustrations. If, at the end of this tale, anyone thinks that "clothes make the man," he is probably wearing a tail.

Retold and illustrated by: Nadine Bernard Westcott
Little, Brown, & Co., 1984. Paperback: $5.95

Other books by this author:
The Giant Vegetable Garden; I Know an Old Lady Who Swallowed a Fly; The Lady with the Alligator Purse; Peanut Butter and Jelly

A Friend Is Someone Who Likes You

Value: Generosity

Joan Walsh Anglund is an artist/writer with very special talents. I especially enjoyed reading her books to children on "Captain Kangaroo" because they are so warm and so basic. This book is a good example of her work. We are by nature social creatures, and every child yearns for friendship. Ms. Anglund extends the boundaries of friendship to include things, trees, a stream, the wind. The illustrations are wonderful, and children will know they have made a friend in Ms. Anglund.

Author and Illustrator: Joan Walsh Anglund
Harcourt, 1958. Hardcover: $9.95

Other books by this author:
The Joan Walsh Anglund Storybook; In a Pumpkin Shell: Mother Goose ABC; Childhood Is a Time of Innocence; Love Is a Special Way of Feeling

4 to 8 Years

Hansel and Gretel

Honor: Caldecott Honor

Value: Courage

The brothers Grimm first presented this story almost
two hundred years ago. It remains as one of their most
enduring tales. This version is closely patterned after
their original, and the lush oil paintings render a realism
that enhances the story. It is a chilling story, as are so
many of the Grimm brothers' works, but the happy,
even joyous, ending will please any young listener.

Retold by: Rika Lesser
Illustrator: Paul O. Zelinsky
Putnam, 1984. Paperback: $7.95

Hey, Al

Honor: Caldecott Medal

We never know we have it so good till we don't have it any more. This story is about all that and so much more. Al and Eddie find they don't want to be birds of a feather. They have each other, and that's quite enough.

Author: Arthur Yorinks
Illustrator: Richard Egielski
Farrar, 1986. Paperback: $4.95

Other books by this author:
Company's Coming; Louis the Fish; Oh, Brother; Ugh;
Whitefish Will Rides Again;
It Happened in Pinsk

If I Ran the Zoo

Honor: Caldecott Honor

Value: Imagination

You ou will never visit a zoo again without thinking about what Dr. Seuss's young Gerald McGrew does when he runs the zoo. Animals from places further than away than the imagination! This is the pure genius of Dr. Seuss, and any child will giggle from animal to animal to animal. That is, if you can hear the child giggling over your laughter!

Author and Illustrator: Dr. Seuss
Random, 1950. Hardcover: $13.00

Other books by this author:
Green Eggs and Ham; The Cat in the Hat; Fox in Socks; Horton Hatches the Egg; If I Ran the Circus; Thidwick, the Big-Hearted Moose; Yertle the Turtle and Other Stories

The Legend of the Bluebonnet

Values: Courage / Generosity

Tomie dePaola, with great artistry, traces the Comanche legend about the origin of the Texas state flower. It is a tale of great sacrifice by a young girl who loves her people more than her greatest and most dearly held possession. It is a lovely and moving story.

Retold and illlustrated by: Tomie dePaola
Putnam, 1983. Paperback: $5.95

Other books by this author:
*The Legend of the Indian Paintbrush; The Lady of Guadalupe;
The Clown of God; Bill and Pete;
The Cloud Book*

Madeline

Honor: Caldecott Honor

Value: Generosity

Ludwig Bemelmans's treasure has enchanted several generations. His illustrations are a tour of sparkling Paris, the opera, Notre Dame, the Tuileries Gardens. It is a delightful experience to share with your member of the latest generation.

Author and Illustrator: Ludwig Bemelmans
Penguin, 1939. Paperback: $4.99

Other books in this series:
Madeline and the Bad Hat; Madeline and the Gypsies; Madeline in London; Madeline's Rescue

Mirette on the High Wire

Honor: Caldecott Medal

Value: Courage

Brava, bravo! What a team, Mirette and the Great Bellini. But it does not happen all at once. How do you find your way to the high wire? Practice, practice, practice! This one recently won the Caldecott Medal, and deservedly so. It is a wonderful, even inspiring story of patience and perserverance.

Author and Illustrator: Emily Arnold McCully
Putnam, 1992. Hardcover: $14.95

Other books by this author:
First Snow; Speak Up, Blanche!; The Evil Spell; Picnic; School; The Grandma Mix-Up; Grandmas at Bat

Miss Nelson Is Missing

Value: Trustworthiness

Miss Nelson is a wonderful, friendly teacher, but, as
so often happens, her classroom children do not know
what a great teacher they have. Until one day they meet
Miss Viola Swamp! The class soon learns to appreciate
Miss Nelson. This is a fine story for an early elementary
school child. Perhaps a good point will be made. The
classrooms of this world are filled with Miss Nelsons,
and they need your help. Reading this story to your
youngster is almost better than anything you could
do at the P.T.A. Of course, you'll want to support your
school's P.T.A., also—our schools need all the help
parents can give. Miss Nelson would appreciate it!

Author: Harry Allard, Illustrator: James Marshall
Houghton, 1977. Paperback: $4.95

Other books by this author: *Miss Nelson Has a Field Day;*
Miss Nelson Is Back; Bumps in the Night; The Cactus Flower Bakery

Mouse Soup

Value: Imagination

Should you ever wish to make mouse soup, you ought to know that it's much tastier when mixed with some mouse stories. In this tale, a wise, wise mouse teaches a mean weasel something about the art of making mouse soup. Much fun.

Author and Illustrator: Arnold Lobel
HarperCollins, 1977. Paperback: $3.50

Other books by this author:
Mouse Tales; Grasshopper on the Road; Owl at Home; Small Pig; Uncle Elephant; Ming Lo Moves the Mountain; The Turnaround Wind; Giant John; Owl at Home; A Treeful of Pigs

Mysterious Tadpole

Who could fail to chuckle over the adventures of Louis and Alphonse? This book is worth its weight in laughs. Whatever you do, please don't weigh Alphonse.

Author and Illustrator: Steven Kellogg
Penguin, 1977. Paperback: $4.99

Other books by this author:
Chicken Little; The Island of the Skog; Pinkerton, Behave!;
A Rose for Pinkerton; Prehistoric Pinkerton

Mystery on the Docks

Honor: Reading Rainbow

Value: Courage

Lots of unseemly rats appear in this story as Eduardo, the famous opera singer, is kidnapped by rodents and held aboard ship. Ralph, the short-order cook and Eduardo's biggest fan, accidentally finds himself entangled. It all works out in the end, with Eduardo enjoying Ralph's cooking and Ralph enjoying Eduardo's singing. Don't you just love happy endings?

Author and Illustrator: Thacher Hurd
HarperCollins, 1983. Paperback: $4.95

Other books by this author:
Axle the Freeway Cat; Little Mouse's Big Valentine; Tomato Soup; Mama Don't Allow: Starring Miles and the Swamp Band

Old Henry

Value: Generosity

I don't know if I can get along with you, you do things differently than I, you have a different attitude than I. You are . . . well, you're different. Aren't we all different from one another? And isn't that a joy? It should not be an obstacle to friendship. Old Henry is different, and that's a put-off for his new neighbors. But as the old saying goes, absence makes the heart grow fonder. This fine book has very positive notions about what to do when we meet someone different from us. I love the illustrations.

Author: Joan W. Blos
Illustrator: Stephen Gammell
William Morrow, 1987. Paperback: $4.95

Other books by this author:
The Grandpa Days; Lottie's Circus; Martin's Hats;
A Seed, a Flower, a Minute, an Hour

Ox-Cart Man

Honor: Caldecott Medal

Value: Self-discipline

Loving New England as I do, I cannot help but love this book. The story is wonderful and accurately portrays life in New England in another time. The illustrations have a primitive quality that's just perfect for the text. Share some history with your child by latching on to this gem.

Author: Donald Hall
Illustrator: Barbara Cooney
Puffin, 1979. Paperback: $4.99

Other books by this author:
The Oxford Book of Children's Verse in America; I Am the Dog; I Am the Cat; The Farm Summer 1942; The Man Who Lived Alone

Paul Bunyan

Honor: Reading Rainbow

Of all tall tales, none, absolutely none, are as tall as the tales of Paul Bunyan. If you ever wondered about the origins of the Saint Lawrence River, the Great Lakes, and the Grand Canyon, look no farther than that well-known fellow. Some call it fiction, but the next time you hear a roar of thunder coming from the northwest, listen closer. That roar has a human quality, and it just may be Paul himself roaring in laughter! Nifty book.

Retold and illustrated by: Steven Kellogg
William Morrow, 1984. Paperback: $5.95

Other books by this author:
Chicken Little; Pecos Bill; Johnny Appleseed; Mike Fink: A Tall Tale; Best Friends; The Island of the Skog

Petunia, Beware!

Value: Trustworthiness

"The grass is always greener," as the old saying goes. Often children display this attitude towards another child's toys or clothes or other belongings. This story shows the foolishness of such an attitude and also shows that danger can lurk in other places.

Author and Illustrator: Roger Duvoisin
Random House, 1958. Paperback: $3.95

Other books by this author:
Petunia; Petunia: The Silly Goose Stories; Petunia's Christmas; Petunia, I Love You; Petunia Takes a Trip; The House of Four Seasons

Pierre

A Cautionary Tale

Value: Fairness

Maurice Sendak is so in touch with childhood, and the proof is this little gem, *Pierre*. How frustrating to hear a child say over and over, "I don't care!" That's what *Pierre* is all about, caring. Read it to a child, and see the flower of caring bloom in front of your eyes.

Author and Illustrator: Maurice Sendak
HarperCollins, 1962. Paperback: $3.95

Other books by this author:
Chicken Soup with Rice; In the Night Kitchen; The Nutshell Library; Where the Wild Things Are; Seven Little Monsters; Outside Over There

Princess Smartypants

This is one smart princess with her mind made up about how she wants to live. None of her would-be suitors can fulfill the tasks she sets them—then along comes Prince Swashbuckle. It's a fun story.

Author and Illustrator: Babette Cole
Putnam, 1986. Paperback: $5.95

Other books by this author:
*Hurrah for Ethelyn; Supermoo!; The Trouble with Mom;
The Trouble with Uncle*

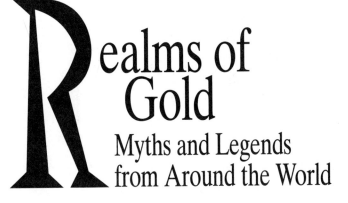

Realms of Gold
Myths and Legends from Around the World

Values: All

Myths are the stuff of which cultures are made, and these myths and legends from many cultures around the world should be a part of any child's education. Besides, they are fun and filled with fascination.

Stories collected by: Ann Pilling
Illustrator: Kady MacDonald Denton
Kingfisher, 1993. Hardcover: $16.95

Another book by this author:
Before I Go to Sleep: Bible Stories, Poems, and Prayers for Children

Rosie and Michael

Values: Fairness / Generosity

If you want to explain to a child what it means to be a friend, try *Rosie and Michael*. Now, that's friendship! With humor and honesty, Rosie and Michael tell you all about their friendship. It's a primer on the subject.

Author: Judith Viorst
Illustrator: Lorna Tomei
Macmillan, 1974. Paperback: $3.95

Other books by this author:
*Alexander and the Terrible, Horrible, No Good, Very Bad Day;
Alexander, Who Used to Be Rich Last Sunday; The Tenth Good Thing about Barney; The Good-Bye Book;
I'll Fix Anthony*

Ruby the Copycat

Values: Fairness / Generosity

Copycatting is a part of every childhood. This is a pleasant little story about a copycat. All works out well. All works out well. Oops!

Author and Illustrator: Peggy Rathmann
Scholastic, 1991. Paperback: $4.95

Other books by this author:
Officer Buckle and Gloria; Good Night, Gorilla

Shoes

Honor: Reading Rainbow

Young children are often fascinated by clothing, and shoes generally top the list. This is a delightful book for young readers beginning their early ed-shoe-cation. The illustrations are pixie-like, just perfect for the subject.

Author: Elizabeth Winthrop
Illustrator: William Joyce
HarperCollins, 1986. Paperback: $4.95

Other books by this author:
Sledding; Bear and Mrs. Duck; Lizzie and Harold; The Best Friends Club: A Lizzie and Harold Story; Katherine's Doll; Maggie and the Monster; A Very Noisy Girl; I'm the Boss

4 to 8 Years

The Sleeping Beauty

Value: Trustworthiness

The familiar Grimm tale from Germany is beautifully retold by Trina Schart Hyman, but it is her illustrations of such color and character and detail that make this a fine work. As one drop of blood puts an entire castle to sleep, so one kiss, a hundred years later, awakens it to live happily ever after. Every child will live happily through this story.

Retold and illustrated by: Trina Schart Hyman
Little, Brown & Co., 1977. Paperback: $6.95

Other books by this author:
Snow White; A Little Alphabet; Little Red Riding Hood